DANGEROUS MEN

Volume 71, Sage Library of Social Research

SAGE LIBRARY OF SOCIAL RESEARCH

Dangerous Men
The Sociology of Parole

Richard McCleary

Foreword by DAVID FOGEL

Volume 71
SAGE LIBRARY OF
SOCIAL RESEARCH

 **SAGE PUBLICATIONS**   Beverly Hills   London

For information address:

SAGE PUBLICATIONS, INC.
275 South Beverly Drive
Beverly Hills, California 90212

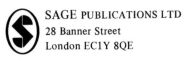

SAGE PUBLICATIONS LTD
28 Banner Street
London EC1Y 8QE

Printed in the United States of America

Library of Congress Cataloging in Publication Data

McCleary, Richard.
Dangerous men: The Sociology of Parole

(Sage library of social research ; v. 71)
Bibliography: p. 177
Includes index.
1. Parole--United States. 2. Recidivists--United States. 3. Corrections--United States. I. Title.
HV9304.M185   364.6'2'0973   78-19859
ISBN 0-8039-1094-0
ISBN 0-8039-1095-9 pbk.

SECOND PRINTING

CONTENTS

ACKNOWLEDGMENTS

I am indebted to Howard S. Becker, Donald T. Campbell, Andrew C. Gordon, and James P. Pitts for long-range help with this essay. During my tenure as a student at the Center for Urban Affairs, each of these people helped me write substantial portions of the book. John L. McKnight lent me a number of ideas, insights, and prejudices which have worked their way into the essay. Sarah Fenstermaker Berk is most responsible for the rigorous logic. Where my logic fails, I am guilty of not following her advice. Finally, I am indebted to the editors of *Social Problems* for permission to use substantial portions of two articles.

FOREWORD

The President's Crime Commission, using 1965 data, reported 2.8 million index crimes in the United States; 727,000 of these crimes were cleared by an arrest but only 177,000 of these arrests resulted in the issuance of a formal charge—and this figure dwindled further when 9,000 cases were dismissed. Of the 168,000 cases actually tried in that year, 8,000 resulted in acquittals. Of those convicted, 56,000 were placed on probation, 6,000 were fined, and 35,000 received short jail sentences; thus 63,000 went to prison. Prison commitments were augmented that year by 21,000 probation violators. If attrition percentages are computed, only 65 percent of all convictions resulted in a prison sentence; only 39 percent of all those tried, 36 percent of all those charged, and only 8 percent of all those arrested were imprisoned; only 2.3 percent of the reported index crimes lead to a prison sentence for the offender. The crime-prison nexus is problematic. When victimization rates for the major cities are added to the reported crime rates, the nexus becomes weaker and more problematic. It is only with the greatest difficulty and imagination that crime and prisoners, or parolees, can be causally associated. The imprisoned group may then be called, in Zimring's words, "a stand-in population." Prisoners represent a very small, random (though not in the scientific sense) sample of offenders.

A sort of Parkinson's Law is also at work here. During busy time, crime waves, that is, the number of prisoners approaches the prison bed capacity in many states. The nexus between

crime and imprisonment is still weak, however. Prison commitment rates are apparently more closely related to unemploy-
ment rates and to prison bed space capacities than to crime
rates. The zenith of prison commitment rates in this century,
for example, was during the Great Depression. During this same
period, contrary to popular belief, crime rates were relatively
stable.

The rate of imprisonment is also related to prison bed space
capacity. As the prisons fill up, the criminal justice system must
slow down. Fortunately, as bed space diminishes, parole boards
may speed up the rate of release through parole, thus freeing up
scarce bed space for incoming prisoners. The criminal justice
system is thus *truly* dynamic, and in this sense, it may be said
that the system per se "produces" the stand-in population of
prisoners. The stand-in population, of course, is the result of a
not so unconscious process of mortification, stripping, and
punishment. In any case, however, the stand-in population
remains a small, representative group of essentially poor, young,
urban, and increasingly darker-skinned males whom we deal
with in the most onerous manner. In the very limited cases of
capital sentences, these demographic characteristics are even
more pronounced. The group finally selected to enter the prisons, and thus, to leave the prisons as parolees, are symbolic
losers in a Darwinian sense.

The reason for such a (perhaps too) lengthy introduction to
this Foreword is to emphasize the nature of the problem. *In
parole, we deal with a stand-in population—a symbolic population.* Strip away the symbolism and these "dangerous men"
become a pathetic group. McCleary's book is above all a treatise
on the symbolic nature of parole, and the image of the dangerous man is only the beginning. Another image is "recidivism."
The "success" or "failure" of our correctional treatment and
parole supervision programs is evaluated on the basis of how
well the symbolic population fares upon release-by-parole. This
evaluative criterion, "recidivism," has become the sole focus of
research in corrections and parole. The recidivism-chasers have
created a myopic view of correctional-parole success attribu-

tion. In this decade, for example, a debate has raged over the magnitude of the *true* recidivism rate. One side argues that *only* one of four parolees actually succeeds. The other side argues that *only* one of four parolees actually fails. Experts on each side argue that their estimate of the recidivism rate is the *true* estimate. But what do these numbers actually mean?

Suppose that the parole-is-working partisans turn out to be correct—only 25 percent of all parolees fail. Suppose further that the situation improves and the recidivism rate approaches 0 percent. Is this an argument for retaining parole as a component of the criminal justice system? And *whose* success is measured by this number: The ex-con's, the parole officer's, the system's, chance, or all of these?

The question of *whose* success or failure is measured by a recidivism rate is further muddled when other criminal justice components are considered. Suppose, for example, that the police improve their arrest function and actually reach the criminal careerists; and that prosecutors gain more convictions; and that judges are able to select only the irredeemable for incarceration. This is an unlikely series of events, but if it were to happen, we would be confronted with a reversal of the success interpretation. Under these conditions, along with a stable or marginal increase in cell space, only the worst of the symbolic lot would be selected for prison stays, thus forming the pool for subsequent parole selection. The more efficient the front-end of the criminal justice system becomes, the closer we come to incarcerating only "real" criminals. Absent the current symbolic residual population, all parolees would remain committed to criminal careers, and thus, we would expect a recidivism approaching 100 percent. Any recidivism rate lower than 100 percent would be interpreted as failure for the police-prosecutor-court function just as any recidivism rate higher than 0 percent is now interpreted as failure for the correctional-parole function. To make everyone happy, of course, we might strive for a recidivism rate of exactly 50 percent. With this number, no one finishes first, but then again, no one finishes last. No criminal justice component is a *total* failure. To achieve this

magical 50 percent recidivism rate, this golden mean, we need
only make sure that prison commitments are a half-and-half mix
of irredeemables and redeemables.

A more realistic solution perhaps is to realize that recidivism
rates are merely numbers with little or no *real* meaning. If there
is a single recurring lesson on this point in McCleary's book, it is
that, indeed, not only is a recidivism rate meaningless, it is a
statistic that the system itself produces. It is thus arbitrary. In
Chapter 2, McCleary shows how parole officers "paper" their
caseloads to maintain a desired number of clients, and not
coincidentally, to inflate the success rates in their caseloads; in
Chapter 3, McCleary shows how the outcomes of individual
cases depend upon the needs of the individual parole officer in
his or her relationship to the larger system; in Chapters 4 and 5,
this lesson is reinforced when parolee classification and record-
keeping functions are considered. Overall, the inescapable conclusion is that recidivism statistics reflect only the concrete
needs and values of the individuals who run the criminal justice
system at the operational lowest level. Parole officers and po-
licemen *need* a certain number of failures and a certain number
of successes to function on a routine, daily basis.

A larger theme in McCleary's study is the notion of the
professional role. Parole supervision is not so much Kafka as it
is Pirendello—a group of professionals in search of a mission.
Many authors have already pointed out the strains involved in
trying to be a cop and a counselor at the same time. The strain
periodically becomes visible. When parole officers in the past
have been threatened with disarmament, they have closed ranks
and stressed the public safety agent, or cop-like aspects of their
roles. The "firearms rebellion" described by McCleary in Chapter 2 is a typical example. But when salary raises are sought
and/or when occupational enhancement becomes a question,
parole officers invariably stress those aspects of their roles that
are professional-like. Role confusion is rampant.

Closer to home (Chicago), but in other jurisdictions as well, a
parole officer can be seen going off to his/her appointed rounds
with Freud in one hand and a .38 Smith and Wesson in the

other hand. It is by no means clear that Freud is as helpful as the .38 in most areas where parole officers venture—at least in the great urban areas of the nation. Is Freud a backup to the .38? Or is the .38 carried to "support" Freud? With revocations increasingly diminishing (see the U.S. Supreme Court ruling in *Morrissey*), and with more jurisdictions moving to a time-limited term of parole either through legislation or administrative order, the vitality of the idea that parole is part of the rehabilitative process is waning. If a person by law is on parole for six to twelve months and is not rehabilitated by that time, what then can a parole officer claim to be doing other than acting as a public safety agent?

Some critics have suggested the abolition of parole supervision except when an ex-convict voluntarily requests the service. This suggestion has been attacked as harsh. Critics charge that it would be something less than humane to dump a man outside the prison wall with $50 gate money and no parole officer to assist the ex-prisoner with reintegration. The abolitionists might agree that, at the core, the problem is not so much the prospective parolee's lost opportunity to avail himself of the parole officer's altruism, but rather, the problem is in the definition of the situation. Prison clinicians require a dominance-submission relationship, and upon release, the ex-prisoner's freedom must be gradual, graduated, and measured. Prisoners call the parole period a "tail," meaning a sort of leash. The leash or tail can snap the body back into prison. In a word, someone else is in control. Just as clinicians inside the prison are in a mild panic about viewing their clientele as volitional, parole authorities are frightened by the prospect of losing control over their parolees. Their humanistic plea to be allowed to assist the prisoner at release is disingenuous because the relationship they require with the parolee is based ultimately upon coercion, to say nothing of the .38 many parole officers pack.

In the final analysis, parole as it now exists is part of the social control mechanism called criminal justice. When McCleary describes the routine duties of a parole officer, he describes techniques of social control. In Chapter 4, where he describes how some parolees become dangerous men, the process of social control is laid bare. The parole bureaucracy cannot even *think* about parolees in the abstract without initiating the social control process.

Some argue that parole should settle for a facilitative role, easing the ex-con's reintegration into the free world. Others believe that the parole officer can be authoritative without being authoritarian, and thus, that the parole officer can effectively counsel. In urban America, it seems to make no difference. Parole officers and their parolees live out ethnologically disparate existences. The former can rarely know what is going on in the lives of the latter, much less *control* what is going on. The state cannot with much confidence hire one person to "treat" another unless the other wants something to happen.

What McCleary describes as bureaucratic *dysfunction* in his study, I prefer to call bureaucratic *injustice*. The implication here is that a more functionally efficient parole bureaucracy will *not* lead to a more fundamentally sound or rational system of parole. Parole as it exists in urban America is per se the source of much that is described by McCleary as bureaucratic dysfunction. It is not dysfunction in the supervision agency that leads to corruption, abuse, and injustice. Rather, it is the fundamentally unjust nature of parole which leads inevitably to dysfunction in the organization charged with parole supervision. Ultimately, McCleary's book must be read as an argument for a justice model of parole.

The *entire* process of corrections needs to be put on the continuum of justice. From the day a man enters prison until he is discharged from parole (if parole is to be continued at all), our efforts should be to enhance the opportunities for responsible choices, *including the option to refuse supervision and the right to face the consequences of one's choices.*

Elsewhere I have recommended a voucher credit (a computerized account) system for the delivery of program services in prisons. If prisoner volition is a viable concept, then most coercive clinical services could be zero-based budgeted. This is especially true in determinate sentencing jurisdictions where

conformance to and/or success in a correctional treatment program do not net the prisoner additional good time credit. For
example, for each day of vested good (lawful behavior) time
which goes into a prisoner's account, we would also award a $6
to $8 credit. (This is to be seen as "computer" money, not
cash.) Prisoners, separately or in groups, could, with prison
counsel, contract for educational, vocational, or clinical services
from private practitioners. Using such a system, or a variation
upon a similar theme, the professionals contracted would be of
a need breed. A prisoner would "employ" his teacher, counsel-
lor, etc. A caseworker would, for example, be prisoner A's
caseworker, not the warden's caseworker. Properly understood,
the contracted professional is an advocate for the prisoner.
Lawyers, socialized in an adversary educational environment,
have less difficulty with this concept of service delivery than do
clinicians who are socialized in a consensus-adjustment training
environment. After all, could a lawyer as a matter of ethics
consider representing both the warden and the prisoner? Clinicians have not fully faced up to this spiritual conflict of interest. For many, their dual role does not even appear as a conflict.

Extending the voucher system to the postincarcerative experience, we visualize a man leaving prison with a niggardly sum of
gate money in cash and the unexpended (or a set sum of, say,
$1500) good time—computer money on account. This sum
might be required to be spent within a specified time frame for
tuition, training, counseling, etc., expenses. The residual role of
the parole officer might simply be to make sure the parolee
does indeed receive the services in the private (or public) sector
agencies for which he contracts, using his voucher account. The
parole officer would at the same time be a *broker* and *advocate*
for his/her voluntary client. He/she would be responsible for
helping the parolee negotiate both a sensible plan of training or
work and chart a course through frequently impenetrable
human service bureaucracies.

I suspect that a voucher system would neutralize the parolee
classification system which McCleary describes in Chapter 4.
The process whereby a parolee becomes a "client" is at best a

random process, set by fortune and by the whim of a parole officer. Yet justice demands that *any* parolee be allowed to become a "client" *if the parolee so wishes.* Or if the parolee wishes not become a "client," a justice perspective demands that too. A voucher plan in this sense would serve as an instrument of social mobility, allowing the parolee some choice in the process. Beyond this, a voucher system would make waves in other areas of the corrections-parole component. Parole supervision meetings themselves might be transformed from painful violations-seeking sessions to more helpful mutual exploration.

An argument against a voucher system (or against the abolition of parole altogether) is that parole provides a valuable public safety mechanism. But this is a false argument. The U.S. Supreme Court (in *Morrissey*) has shifted the traditional parole officer-parolee revocation relationship, based as it was upon technical violation (or the obfuscation of actual crimes), to the police-parolee prosecution relationship, based upon new crimes. The data are clear on this. Since *Morrissey,* parolees are rarely returned to prison for any offense less than a new crime. The police officer has replaced the parole officer as the primary agent of parole revocation and this is probably the way it ought to be. Public safety is the police officer's *metier* anyhow. This leaves the parole officer free to practice some other role, preferably one that is useful and consistent with a justice model. The father of the indeterminate sentence and parole supervision in America, Zebulon Brockaway, long ago suggested this two-pronged strategy when in 1912 (*Fifty Years of Prison Service,* p. 324) he said:

> The most satisfactory [person] for supervision of paroled men is the chief of police; not the average policeman in the great cities, nor indeed a religious or philanthropic organization or private individual. Certified pecuniary prosperity, the result of legitimate industry and economy, was the prized favorable indication of rectitude.

And this brings us back to the notion of success. Finding a job and stability is after all as much as we might expect from a man trying to overcome the deterioration which usually accompanies a prison sentence. Less elegantly put, set parole officers to the task of helping the parolee find a job and set the police to the task of keeping an eye on the parolee.

David Fogel

DAVID FOGEL is a Professor of Criminal Justice at the University of Illinois, Chicago Circle. He attended Brooklyn College, the University of Dijon, France, the University of Minnesota, Columbia University, and the University of California, Berkeley. Dr. Fogel writes from a wide and varied background in criminal justice. He has served as Executive Director of the Illinois Law Enforcement Commission, as Commissioner of the Minnesota Department of Corrections, and as Superintendent of the Marin County (California) Juvenile Hall. Dr. Fogel has published extensively in social science journals but he is best known for his book, *We Are the Living Proof: The Justice Model for Corrections.*

Chapter 1

INTRODUCTION

This is an empirical study of an unnamed parole agency. The focus of the study is *sociological* because, as it turns out, the dangerous men who give this book its name are dangerous only in a *sociological* sense. To illustrate this, consider how Sutherland and Cressy (1970: 584) define parole:

> the status of being released from a penal or reformatory institution in which one has served a part of his maximum sentence, on condition of maintaining good behavior and remaining in the custody and under the guidance of the institution or some other agency approved by the state until a final discharge is granted.

If this definition has a crucial phrase at all, it must be "good behavior," that mode of conduct which the parolee is expected to maintain in return for continued freedom. On the face of it, men released from prison are bound by a parole contract wherein the standards of acceptable conduct are made explicit. Except for the most obvious sorts of misbehavior, however, such as committing a new crime or absconding, these standards are vague. Dangerous men are seldom distinguishable from run-of-the-mill parolees on the basis of these criteria alone. Behavior is defined as "good" or "bad" only through a complicated social process which operates independently of absolute criteria. Traditional studies of parole have concentrated on statistical analyses of recidivism. Glaser's (1964) monumental study of the Federal parole system is typical of the genre. Parole outcome, success or failure, is defined as a dependent variable with parolee characteristics and contexts defined as causors. The parole experience in this genre is seen as a sort of *ceteris paribus* experiment where outcome is *caused* by a set of independent variables. Parolees succeed or fail only because a set of antecedant conditions favor that outcome.

This genre has been closely identified with and/or attributed to the positivist school of criminology. The causal prescriptions of the genre have been applied most widely under the rubric of "rehabilitation." In recent years, however, the questions and answers generated by the traditional theories have been judged unsatisfactory on a number of grounds. There have, nevertheless, been no coherent, compelling alternatives to the traditional sociologies of parole.

My own work (McCleary, 1975; 1977), the work of Takagi (1967; Takagi and Robison, 1968), and the work of Prus and Stratton (1976) have taken a novel approach with limited and differential results. With respect to parole statistics, for example, I have found it profitable to examine the interests of the statistics producer, that is, the interests of the people who work in the parole agency. If parole outcomes are a function of the interests at play in the agency, then the frequency of an outcome depends upon how well that outcome fits into the plans of the people who work in the agency. An outcome that disrupts the status quo is likely to be rare, while outcomes that fit neatly into the existing scheme of things are likely to be common.

To illustrate this principle in the limited context of recidivism statistics, consider what might happen if a parole agency decided that failures could occur only on Fridays. The failures would occur ad libitum, of course, for the agency cannot control the many factors that underlie the time of failure. But the agency might require a failure to be instigated by a formal complaint and might require that all formal complaints be made on Fridays.

This did happen in the parole agency which serves as the basis for this study. Whereas prior to 1975 the parole officers working for the agency could file complaints on any day of the week at any time of the day, the new policy set aside Friday afternoons for this exclusive purpose. The new policy brought about an abrupt drop in the number of "nuisance" or technical violation complaints filed against parolees. What happened here, of course, is that the new policy cut into the number of three-day weekends available to agency employees. A complaining parole officer could still file "nuisance" complaints against parolees for whatever reason, but the new policy set a cost for this behavior. If business were to continue as usual, there would have to be an adjustment in the work and life styles parole officers had defined for themselves. And of course, the statistical signature of this new policy was an abrupt drop in the frequency of parole failures or recidivism.

Now this is an extreme example and one that addresses only a narrow topic: the validity of recidivism statistics. The causal nexus in this illustration is obvious and the social basis is clear. In other contexts, the situation will be subtler. Overall, the phenomena described in later chapters might be missed or misinterpreted by the casual, untrained observer. The parole agency, after all, is a complex, formal organization whose routine activity overwhelms the senses. Interpreting this activity can be likened to interpreting the activity of a beehive. The untrained observer will miss or misinterpret phenomena that the entymologist will not miss.

Of course, there is another difference between the casual observer and scientist: the scientist is informed by a body of theory. Theory focusses and organizes a set of otherwise unfocussed observations. The sociology of parole is informed by the body of theory dealing with the formation and functioning of formal organizations. A parole agency is a formal organization, and parole outcomes are the output of a bureaucratic dynamic.

I have more to say about the bureaucratic dynamic, but it will be useful to first consider the historical forces at play. It is a fact that the long-term trend in the administration of parole has been in the direction of formalization or bureaucratization. In the nineteenth century, where it existed at all, parole was administered by individuals or by informal groups. Parole at the Elmira Reformatory circa 1880, for example, was handled by the reformatory superintendent. Parolees reported in person to the superintendent on the first of each month. At the end of six months, the superintendent certified the parolee as reformed and discharged him from supervision. The superintendent alone decided who was to be paroled and there were no appeals.

Informality was possible in this situation, first, because the superintendent controlled the parole decision-making process. Only model prisoners were considered for parole. And second, the superintendent never had more than a few parolees to worry about at any given time. In contrast, modern parole agencies supervise thousands of parolees simultaneously. Further, many of these parolees, perhaps even the majority, would not have been eligible for parole in earlier days.

More important than this straightforward increase in scale, however, is the increased complexity of the role played by parole in the criminal justice system. At Elmira, the superintendent's duties were quite simple. But as times change, the role of the supervision agency becomes more complicated and demanding. A modern parole agency is expected not only to supervise, but also to diagnose, classify, and certify parolees; to keep records for other formal organizations, such as the courts; to rehabilitate parolees; to monitor and evaluate the effectiveness of rehabilitation programs; with the 1971 U.S. Supreme Court decision in *Morrissey versus Brewer,* a more sophisticated role was thrust upon parole agencies. *Morrissey* demanded that agencies protect the due process rights of parolees, and in this respect, *Morrissey* had the same effect on parole agencies that *Miranda* has had on police departments.

According to the most widely accepted theories, formalization or bureaucratization is the likely response of informal social units to an increasingly complicated environment. Formal organizations arise precisely because their functions have become too cumbersome or complicated to be performed by the simpler social unit. But the subsequent growth of the formal organization is not so clearly a response to need. Once a formal organization becomes entrenched in the socio-political environment, it may grow regardless of the need.

Now returning to the subject of bureaucratic dynamics, this unjustified growth is the kernel of the problem. Gordon et al. (1974) speak of the social service bureaucracy as a self-serving, self-generating organism:

> There is available on many toy counters an unusual and instructive machine. It is a battery-operated five-inch box with a lid and an exposed switch. It is otherwise unadorned. If someone flips the switch to turn the machine on, a grotesque hand emerges from beneath the lid with a single purpose: to turn the switch "off" again so that the machine can sit silently until someone else turns it back "on." . . . In one sense, this is a perfect machine. The hand effectively carries out its mission—to prevent any outside interference with whatever is going on inside the box. . . . Imagine a bureaucracy which is similarly perfect, one which operates only in ways that guarantee its continued smooth operation and does not brook interference from the outside world.

The self-serving, self-generating "box" serves as a metaphor for what I have called the bureaucratic dynamic. It is a "black box" because the internal process can be observed only in terms of inputs and outputs, that is, in terms of the men released from prison and their parole outcomes.

Now formal organizations theory is typically concerned with describing and explaining the "black box." In particular, theory addresses the effect of *structure* on input/output chains, attributing various patterns of bureaucratic phenomena to various types of bureaucratic structures. Merton (1936; 1940), Selznick (1949), and Gouldner (1954), among others, have developed theories to explain bureaucratic *dysfunction*. However, each of these theories requires a level of understanding which is lacking in this sociology of parole.

Most formal organizations, for example, are goal-oriented. When this is the case, dysfunction can be measured as the nonattainment of goals. The organization whose goals are well defined can innovate, and in the long run, an innovative organization is more adaptable. In one sense, we might say that parole agencies have two goals: to rehabilitate those parolees who are amenable to rehabilitation while simultaneously protecting society from those parolees who are not. But this appears to be an oversimplification of the matter. The legitimate goals of any parole agency are more ambiguous, and worse, more variant with time than the goals of, say, businesses, schools, hospitals, and other formal organizations.

It is precisely this degree of ambiguity and inconsistency which rules out formal organizations theory for a sociological analysis of parole. At a later point, for example, I make use of Merton's *goal displacement* concept. But my use of this rich theoretical tool is limited to a narrow context where a goal happens to be well-defined and thus displaceable. In wider contexts, such theories are only marginally useful. The nature of parole is such that its sociology must become empirical in the crudest sense. In what follows, so far as possible and practicable, "the data speak for themselves."

A Description of the Research Method

The parole agency used for this study is the large metropolitan division of a state Department of Corrections (hereafter: DC). There are six branch offices of the DC metropolitan division. Each branch office is housed in a separate building. A branch office ordinarily serves the precincts in its immediate neighborhood.

Data collection began in September 1974. I had selected the general topic of parole for a class in research methods. As the project was for academic "practice" only, entry into the field was casual and unplanned. I called the branch office nearest my home and spoke to the office supervisor. I explained my project, and he was neither enthusiastic nor encouraging but suggested that I meet with him. I arrived at the branch office the next day, and after a short discussion with the supervisor, was given permission to interview the parole officers (hereafter, *POs*) who were in the office at that time. I spoke to three POs that afternoon but took no notes of the conversations. At the end of the afternoon, the supervisor suggested that I seek formal permission from the DC Director to continue my project. I did this, and within the next week, was given a formal letter of permission. The terms of my agreement with the Director were that I would not seek access to "clinical" data and that I would not misrepresent myself to anyone. In return, I was permitted to interview all consenting DC employees.

In retrospect, it appears that data collection proceeded in three rough phases. The first phase, lasting approximately six months, consisted largely of interviewing POs, supervisors, and DC officials in their offices. I encountered little resistance from POs or from supervisors in this phase of the study. I suspect that one reason for my success in this respect was my role as an organizational outsider. There are strong norms in the branch offices against criticizing the casework of another PO. As an outsider, however, I was a convenient neutral audience. Similarly, supervisors who otherwise had no one to "explain things" to, seemed to enjoy giving me their interpretations of the phenomena I had observed. I suspect also that many POs and supervisors were motivated largely by curiosity. As often as not, they posed questions to me. When their questions touched on the other offices or the discussions I had had with other actors, I demurred. Later, it appeared that this strategy was the correct one. A number of actors told me that they would not have answered my questions unless they had been convinced that their answers would be treated confidentially.

At the end of six months, I had interviewed over fifty people and was satisfied with my knowledge of the actors and of the office routines. The single point of dissatisfaction was my knowledge of the DC officials. With only a few exceptions, my knowledge of these actors was indirect and second-hand. I also had little direct knowledge of the PO-parolee interaction. This did not trouble me because, at that time, I believed that POs would behave in the field much the same way they behaved in their offices. This notion turned out to be incorrect. During the second phase of data collection, also lasting approximately six months, I went out into the field with POs and discovered that their behavior was totally different outside of the office.

My entry into the field was accidental. I had been trying to gain access to the DC training academy but with little success. The DC officials who were in charge of this facility either turned down my requests directly or managed systematically to avoid me. I told one branch office supervisor of my experiences in this area and he suggested that I go out into the field with his POs. The DC training academy is run strictly on a "school" format, emphasizing paperwork and routines. After graduation, novice POs are given field experience in the branch offices and this field experience is considerably more important. My role during this second phase consisted of participant observation but of the type that Gold (1958) calls "the observer as participant." The POs I accompanied into the field knew me and thus knew that I was not a novice PO. There was no initial awkwardness, however, and in most cases, the POs were happy to have some company in the field.

During the first phase, my field notes consisted mainly of question and answer transcripts reproduced from memory. My second phase field notes were similar in format but the questions were usually prompted by observations. For example, A PO might do something that I could not understand, so later, I would ask him to explain what he had done. I also began to review my earlier field notes and was struck by a number of misimpressions or inconsistencies: What POs do is not always the same as what they say they do. I was able to clear up the misimpression or inconsistency in every case by returning to the source.

I also had more success with DC officials during this phase. There are two possible reasons for this. First, I had acquired a knowledge of routines, and hence, was able to "accidentally" meet a number of DC officials outside of their offices. Second, I had acquired an insider's knowledge of the bureaucracy and was able to ask insider's questions. As these questions ordinarily related to areas of policy and accountability, many administrators felt it in their best interests to "set me straight." Finally, in a few cases, I had uncovered information that was personally embarrassing to the administrator and there is little doubt that the administrators suffered my questions in these cases only in return for my silence. This would not have been necessary.

In the spring of 1976, a report of this study appeared in a journal. About two weeks later, I was working late at night in a branch office with a PO. We had just completed a series of field visitations and were completing the required paperwork. A DC official walked into the office, saw us working, and then walked out again. The next day, the PO's records were audited and he was officially reprimanded for trivial irregularities in his records. The causal nexus was obvious. The PO had not been reprimanded for record-keeping irregularities, the official reason, but rather, for being seen with me. The second phase of the study ended at this point.

The third phase of data collection, lasting approximately one year, used informants. I had developed close working relationships with a number of POs by this time and was able to keep up with the daily routines through informal contact. I spoke with at least one PO from each branch office weekly. The conversation was sometimes face-to-face but more often by telephone and normally lasted for an hour or more. I had developed definite theories about the bureaucratic dynamic and posed questions within this framework. Moreover, as I had absorbed the work *ethos* by this time, communication with my informants was efficient. I was able to ask specific and pointed questions about the actors and routines. I concentrated on theoretically interesting cases during this phase, "tracking" the cases through the various bureaucratic processes. The outcomes of these interesting cases often confirmed my theories, but in some cases indicated that the theory was incorrect. This method of "proof" is analytic induction, as described by Becker (1963), and suffers from the logical constraints posed by inductive reasoning as well as the substantive constraints posed by the data.

A Day in the Life

(*What follows is an actual interview written up in the first
week of June, 1976. Naturally, the interview as presented here
has been edited so as not to include any identifiers. I prefer
making notes during the actual conversation. The notes are then
used as a mnemonic device for reproducing the conversation.
This is not always possible because some POs are annoyed or
bothered by note taking. Other POs seem not to mind, or at
least, understand the necessity. Bob, the PO who speaks in this
interview, has told me this explicitly. Because I was able to take
notes, my conversations with Bob are of a better quality than
the average. I have shown him this particular interview and he
agreed that this is more or less what he said.*

(*I can give a brief description of Bob here without identifying
him. He is a "typical" PO—at least demographically. He has an
undergraduate degree in a social science and is currently en-
rolled in a psychiatric social work graduate program. His future
plans are uncertain, but after the M.S.W., he would like to stay
with the DC "if possible." By this, Bob means that he expects
the DC to promote him to a position where he can utilize his
academic credentials.*

(*Bob is in his late twenties, black, and has lived most of his
life in the city. His parole district coincides roughly with the
neighborhood he grew up in. Not surprisingly, a number of his
childhood friends are now his parolees. Bob has commented on
this fact a number of times. He attributes his relative success in
life to a positive family, religion, and fortune: "I was one of the
lucky ones."*

(*On the evening of this conversation, I met Bob in a restaurant near his office. We talked for less than an hour about his
workday. We then went out into the field, and after two hours,
adjourned to a tavern. The conversation at that time was more
general. The conversation begins at approximately five in the
afternoon, and counting the interruption, lasts until ten at
night. Bob speaks:*)

My vice is letting things go until the last minute. You know, never do today what you can put off until tomorrow. Well, today was tomorrow.

First I had a site investigation report to file. The deadline was today. I got down to the office about nine and Terry was already waiting for the report. His deadline was tomorrow. I gave him my standard excuse and asked him to give me a hand with it. He complained about it, you know how he is, but he agreed to help. He really doesn't mind. I help him out sometimes too. Everybody in the office does. So we split the report up. I took the home investigation and he took the employment investigation. He can handle that by phone. All he has to do is call the employer and verify the job. The home investigation is different. You usually can't do that by phone, and even if you could, Terry wouldn't let you. He's a pretty liberal supervisor but that's one rule he won't bend. If he even suspects you didn't visit the home, he'll make you do the report over.

(*The PO training manual is explicit on this point: "The PO must conduct this investigation in the residence where the client plans to reside." Supervisors enforce this rule to the letter. The reason for this is that, or so supervisors believe, a knowledge of the home environment often gives the PO some control over his parolee.*)

I had my car this morning. The address was on_____street, near the el tracks. I couldn't find a parking place nearby, so I parked in front of a loading zone sign. I've got a little Sheriff's Department card that says, "Official Vehicle." I put that on my dash and I usually don't get a ticket. The house was a lower flat, kind of depressed looking. There were vacant lots on both sides and a lot of trash. It was fairly nice looking on the inside, though. The hallway corridor was clean.

The dude I was investigating planned to live at that address with his sister and brother-in-law. You get problems with those arrangements. Sometimes the relatives don't want the dude but they're either afraid to tell him so or else the dude won't take No for an answer. I get some cases where the relatives tell the dude No right out but then the dude thinks they'll change their minds after he moves in. Well, you have to make sure the relatives want the dude.

I knocked on the door a couple of times and the sister answered. She's in her thirties, I'd say and she was dressed neatly, not flashy. She asked to see my ID before she let me in. All in all, she gave me a pretty good first impression. She's a very good housekeeper, very tidy.

All I needed for the report was basic information. A site investigation shouldn't be too long anyway. I started rapping with her and wrote notes down for my report. She's the dude's oldest sister and that's good. Older sisters are like substitute mothers. They have an obligation. Also, the dude's likely to listen to his older sister. Her husband works at the____mill in maintenance. He's been there for three years. That's good too. Shows stability on his part and some insulation. They don't lay maintenance men off. All in all, the family looked good. They're country baptist niggers—and I don't mean that in a bad way because that's what my family was.

Well, I gave her my standard rap and drove back to the office. It was almost eleven by the time I got there. Terry was gone but he had the job investigation done. I looked over his notes and everything seemed to check out alright. It was a fairly good job. I don't expect too much trouble from this dude.

(*POs calculate expectations on the basis of history, job, and home. By the time the site investigation is completed, the PO has a fairly well set expectation of the parolee.*)

I got my notes together with Terry's and turned them over to Alice (*the office receptionist*). She writes up most of my reports. I pay her ten bucks a month for that. I probably wouldn't have to pay her but I want to. That way she's obligated, and of course, I feel better about it. She does a good job in that office. If it weren't for her, I'd have to spend an extra day every week writing and filing. She even signs reports for me—in my handwriting. Now where can you get that for ten bucks a month?

Just as I was getting ready to leave, Chuck came in. He wanted me to cover his office hours next week. Chuck has hours on Friday mornings and I have hours on Friday afternoons. All you really do when you have office hours is sit around, so sometimes we'll cover each other by taking the whole day. Personally, I'd rather work a whole day than two half-days. I'm writing my thesis draft now, so I don't mind doing office hours. It gives me a chance to get my reading and writing done. I told Chuck I'd cover his office hours if he'd cover me in court next Wednesday. He agreed.

(*Covering arrangements are quite common in the branch offices. A PO may have a duty that, while requiring only a few minutes of his time, disrupts his day. If two POs have minor chores on the same day and in the same place, one will cover for the other. Bob explains this:*)

One of my clients is going in front of Judge Kraft next Wednesday. I have to observe the case and write a report on it. Whenever a parolee goes to court, a DC representative has to be there. Now the thing about court is that your case might be scheduled for ten in the morning, and you'll have to be there then, but it won't be called until two in the afternoon. So it wrecks your whole day. What Chuck'll probably do is find out what other DC cases are coming before Kraft Wednesday. Then he'll cover those cases too and the POs will owe him one. To give you an example, I had five cases in court last month. That's five days I would have lost. Instead, I only spent one day in court. The other four days were covered for me.

(*Covering is undoubtedly against the rules. Supervisors do not enforce these rules, however. Restrictions on these informal arrangements will be discussed in later chapters.*)

I left the office at noon and went out to lunch with Dr.____from____University. He's writing a book on psychological systems in parole—which is what my thesis is about. We're helping each other out. He had a copy of one of his chapters and we went over it. His writing style is too scientific for my tastes. He's a brilliant man, though. I suggested that he sit in on one of our group therapy sessions in the office. He has a few questions that I think would be answered by listening to the group rap. He's going to try to make it next Thursday night.

By the time we finished, it was three o'clock. I had some odds and ends left to do, so I want back to the office. For messages and things like that, I usually just call in. Alice has my home and school numbers, so if something important comes up, she can get in touch with me. Otherwise I just call in a couple of times a week. That's the nice thing about this job. Sometimes I don't go into the office for maybe two weeks. Well, there was a message in my box from Freddie Jones. You know Freddie? The junkie? He wanted me to be in the office tomorrow at one so he could call me. Now I happen to know that Freddie's in county jail, so if he's got access to a telephone, there's a security breach down there—or else Freddie's escaped. I took the message to Terry and explained what was up. He got on the phone to a sergeant he knows down at the jail. Freddie's still there. When he tries to use the phone tomorrow, they'll be waiting for him. Things like that are important because we want to get along with the jail people.

(*Informal relationships between the DC and other criminal justice agencies are discussed in later chapters. Note here that the PO is legally bound to report information formally, but that instead, the matter was handled informally by the supervisor.*)

Freddie's nothing but trouble. I don't know what he wanted but it was probably some hustle. He's ripped me off before. Sometimes I wish he'd put the arm on an old lady or something so I could revoke him. He's just a petty thief, though, and he never gets caught. This beef he's in on now is a misdemeanor. It's pretty hard to revoke him for that. What I'm going to do is process him for a drug treatment program,_____. I've got most of the paperwork done on it. As soon as he gets out of jail, I'm getting rid of him.

Well, anyway, I had some odds and ends to take care of at the office. The month ends next week and I've got about five (*routine monthly*) reports to finish. Those don't take any time really but I like to get them done a few days early so that Terry can look them over before he signs them. I spent maybe fifteen minutes finishing those up. Terry made some joke about how I was late on the site investigation report but made it up on these. Then we just talked for about fifteen or twenty minutes. Nothing important. I like to talk to Terry. We're pretty close friends, I think.

Anyway, I got a lot done today. I've got two more site investigations for next month. I'm going to put those off for awhile. One of them looks like it'll require a little extra work. I've got about a week off now. I've got to spend next Friday in the office but there's nothing due before then. I'm going to a party tomorrow night but I'll probably spend the rest of my free time working on the thesis. That's the biggest thing in my life now. Once I get that done, I'll have a better idea about where I'm going. Naturally, I'm not interested in working a district the rest of my life.

(It is now after six, so we pay our bills and leave. Bob has only two stops planned for this evening. POs often refer to this part of their work as "house calls" or "visitations." There are no rules or regulations specifying how many visitations a PO must make with each client; they are not required on any routine basis. POs usually schedule visitations only where they suspect "trouble." In this case, our first visitation is at the home of a parolee who, or so Bob suspects, has absconded. Bob has been unable to contact his parolee by telephone for over a month. The parolee is home. Bob's suspicions have proved false, so we spend only a few minutes on this stop. Had the parolee not been home, we might have talked to one of the parolee's neighbors. Our second stop is with one of Bob's special clients. Bob has taken a personal interest in this parolee. We spend over an hour here, mainly socializing. When we leave, we go to a tavern to continue our conversation. My first question is something like, "What do you like best about your job?" and Bob's answer is:)

The schedule, of course. I work a good fifteen to twenty hours per week but I do it the way I want. That's important. I like counseling too, or just working with people, but the time schedule is the most attractive thing about this job. When I was in the service, I was a clerk in the military police. I had to sit at a desk all day long but I liked it because it was an eight hour job. When the eight hours were up, I was on my own. I like this job for the opposite reason. I don't have to put in a routine shift day after day. This is like being self-employed. Actually, it's more like a profession. I deliver a service, and as long as the quality of the service is good, nobody asks me how much time it took. It might only take me fifteen minutes to straighten out a client, but that's because I'm applying skills and techniques

that took me years to learn. That's what the DC is paying
for—not my time, but my skills.

I read an article in *Federal Probation* once about a time and
motion study of Federal POs. You can't do that in our agency
because we're working under a different philosophy. I kept a
diary for a month once and it only came out to about forty
hours of what most people would call "work." But that's
because of the definition. Look at what I do in a month. I write
up over seventy (*routine monthly*) reports, about two or three
discharges, and four or five site investigations. The total time
for that is only about fifteen hours.

(*I interrupt Bob to question his arithmetic.*)

That's only bookwork. I could probably write all seventy
monthly reports in one morning if I had to. A discharge report
only takes ten minutes. They're all the same. And a site investigation, like the one this morning, shouldn't take more than an
hour. The home investigation is really for my benefit and I have
the home environment sized up in ten minutes. Like the one
this morning, I knew after talking to the lady for five minutes
that it was a good home. Well, maybe I spend twenty hours a
month on those things but not any more than that.

My point is that this job has more to it than just those things.
I have two or three court appearances a month and two or three
revocation hearings usually. But those things don't take long
either. All of my revocations are for new crimes and the police
handle that. I don't have to do any investigations or anything
like that. So let's say I spend a full day in court every month
and another two or three half days at revocation hearings.
Altogether, that only comes to about fifty hours. But returning
to my point, there's more to this job than that.

For one thing, I run a group therapy session once a week.
The DC doesn't pay me anything extra for that. Of course, I'm
using the sessions for data for my thesis, but still, the DC is
getting my time.

Another thing is that I'm on call twenty-four hours a day.
Last week a cop called me at two in the morning to let me
know that one of my clients got picked up. I had to go down to
the station early in the morning to get it cleared up. What the

public doesn't see is the many interfaces with other departments. A PO has to be negotiator. You run into problems with other departments all the time and you really have to solve them on your own. And finally, you have to realize that many of the problems I run into won't fit into an eight-hour day. I'm working right now. I'm thinking about Freddie—what to do with him. That's actually the regular situation. I'm constantly thinking about my caseload. That's something that you have to take into consideration with the (*routine monthly*) reports too. It only takes me a few minutes to write one of those but that's because I've been thinking about the client all month.

(*Our evening ends at this point. My notes of this conversation consist of a few pages of hand-written key words. The key-word for this last paragraph, for example, is "eight-hour day." Early the next morning, I use these hand-written notes to reproduce our conversation as it appears here.*)

Caveat

So far, the methodological description has been obligatory. I intend this introductory chapter to be a *caveat emptor,* however, which means roughly, "Let the buyer beware." Pejorative commercial connotations notwithstanding, this warning implies that I am selling something. If you were buying an automobile from me, you would expect product defects to reveal themselves shortly after purchase. But this is because (and only because) you would be driving and testing the car daily. If the car remained in your garage, on the other hand, undriven and untested, product defects would remain undiscovered.

What I am selling here is a theory about how a parole bureaucracy works. Unlike new cars, theories often remain untested. The major source of defects in any theory can be attributed to perspective, and in this particular case, the theoretical perspective has two facets. First, the facet that comes from the outside, and second, the facet that comes from the inside. The outside perspective is nondenominational social scientific. I mean by this that I have made no value judgments that I am conscious of. Upon reading a portion of this manuscript,

however, an insider complained: "Dammit! There's nothing in
here that isn't true—but it's the *tone* of this thing. You're
making the DC look like a corrupt organization. You've ignored
the positive aspects. Didn't you find anything good at all to
write about?"

All insiders who reviewed the manuscript made a similar
complaint, but in most cases, only about *parts* of the study.
POs, for example, felt that I had described supervisors and DC
officials accurately but had described POs in an inaccurate and
malicious way. DC officials and supervisors reacted similarly.

The second perspectival facet comes from viewing phenomena from the PO's perspective. A major theme running throughout this study is the difference between formal and informal
operations and policies. My knowledge of the formal policy is
considerably less than my knowledge of informal policy mainly
because I have relied on the opinions of the lower level actors.
Policy is written at the highest levels of the bureaucracy, of
course. For example, a high DC official questioned a description
of an official policy as I had described it. In my defense, I
quoted two official DC documents. The official replied: "You
have to realize that the code book was written by lawyers and
was meant to be read by lawyers. You don't have a law degree,
so you're not qualified to read it. I can have a legal opinion
written up for you. Meanwhile, I suggest that you delete this
passage."

The official never delivered the opinion to me, nor did I
delete the offending passage. I confess, however, that my descriptions of "official" or "formal" policy are the descriptions
understood by lower level actors and by myself from readings
of official documents. However, my descriptions are de facto
official because, regardless of absolute meanings, a policy is
defined by the manner in which the lower level actors execute
it.

The insider/outsider biases are not necessarily distinct. Their
interaction is best illustrated by a typical comment from a PO:
"I know who this PO you're talking about here is. It's Jerry.
You know, what you could do is write another chapter com-

paring me to Jerry. The way it is now, you're giving people the impression that all POs are like Jerry."

In fact, the insiders who reviewed portions of this manuscript saw their peers but not themselves. This immediately betrays a scientific outsider bias. In the next chapter, I define POs, supervisors, and DC officials as *classes,* and thus by implication, I ignore the personal differences and interests of the actors. I then betray an insider's bias by outlining the interests of the three classes as I understand them. Naturally, many actors will have personal interests that overwhelm the interests shared with other members of their class. As abstraction is the valid goal of science, however, I have not detailed personal differences and interests except where they illustrate an interest that is general to *all* POs or *all* supervisors or *all* DC administrators. To be sure, there are a few saints and a few sinners in the bureaucracy and I apologize to them for not accurately portraying their behavior.

Perspectival biases should not be understated. They are important and should not be dismissed simply because they are unavoidable. I am convinced that my analysis represents an even balance between my two conscious perspectives; however, I do not believe that I "went native" sometime during the course of the study, nor I hope, have I trivialized my conclusions by suppressing those understandings which are inconsistent with conservative scientific doctrine. Of course, this judgment is left to the reader and to those researchers who might care to validate my work.

In addition to global perspectival biases, the data should be examined with a view to more limited sources of biases. These sources are covered only in an obligatory manner here, and naturally, they are the sources of bias which have been traditional concerns of the scientific community. And naturally, they are the sources of biases which were dealt with a priori.

Sampling. While I spent some time in every branch office and spoke to nearly every PO and supervisor, 90 percent of my time during the first two phases of data collection was spent in only three branch offices and with only twenty-five POs. The POs were selected on the basis of their association with one of the branch offices, that is, the branch office was selected. The three branch offices, moreover, were selected primarily for convenience. One of the offices, for example, happened to be only a few blocks from a freeway exit, so by concentrating on this office, I was able to minimize travel time. The time I spent in the other branch offices, while minimal, convinced me that the interesting phenomena were general from office to office.

Motives. Many POs have told me things that, were the tables turned, I would not have told them. I was initially amazed by their candor but later grew accustomed to it. This change in me was no doubt due to my growing understanding of the situation. This does not explain the initial candor of the actors, however.

One explanation relates to my role as an outsider. In every branch office, there is a strictly enforced noninterference norm. A PO is not allowed to criticize the case decisions of his office-mates. As an outsider, however, I was a convenient neutral audience. Quite often a PO would tell me how a given case "should have been handled." Conversations of this nature gave the PO an opportunity to exhibit his professional knowledge and skills that was otherwise lacking. The PO could not express his concerns to his office-mates because of the norms and could not express his concerns to an outsider, say a bartender, because the bartender would not understand the situation. As my reputation for ethical confidentiality grew, this factor became more important.

This motive gains more weight when my experiences with DC officials are considered. I had little success with administrators during the initial phases of the study. While there are other explanations for this, I am sure that these actors had no need of an outsider in the same sense that the POs did.

A second motive, common to POs, supervisors, *and* DC administrators, was education. I often misunderstood "what had happened" or even "why" and many of the actors were concerned that my misunderstanding would show them up in a bad light: "That's not the right way to do it but it's not the wrong way either. You have to know why I want it done that way. When you see why, then you'll see that it's really not wrong. You've got to use common sense when you interpret the regulations. Now here's what really happens."

With only a few exceptions, my interviews with DC officials were precipitated by basic "misunderstandings" of phenomena. A related motive concerns my growing role as an insider. In the second phase of data collection, for example, POs often answered my questions frankly because they believed that I "already knew" the answer. This was true in some cases and not true in other cases. Whatever, it was apparent to me that many POs spoke candidly simply because, after a certain point in the study, I knew enough about the general situation to know whether I was being lied to or misled.

On this point, my outsider role gave me some status with a powerful clique of POs. The clique, as described in the next chapter, promoted an ideology that was positive towards research, social science, and universities. Of course, no clique member would want to be accused of lying to or misleading a social science researcher who was affiliated with a prestigious university. However, while I took advantage of this motive wherever it existed, I did not attempt to coerce POs into cooperation by appealing to the clique.

All of these motives are understandable to me. I was also pleased to discover during the second phase that some POs had indeed lied to or misled me, and in every case, with a motive that I could understand. For example, many POs exaggerated their educational credentials or the amount of time spent at "work." Had I asked POs how often they changed their underwear, I would have expected some exaggeration too and I would have understood their motives for exaggerating.

But in many cases, I could not understand the motive, or in the extreme, suspected some ulterior motive. On more than one occasion, for example, I suspect that actors gave me information and documents that, for personal reasons, they wanted published. As I had demonstrated my ethical confidentiality to the POs, many saw me as a convenient shield between themselves and the media. Some DC officials saw my research product as an exposé of corruption, and when it suited their purposes to expose the corruption of other DC officials, they gave me documents. In one case, a DC official gave me a set of official-looking documents and then gave my name to a newspaper reporter.

The problem with data obtained under these circumstances is that it is not representative. In the first place, it misrepresents the situation per se. A DC official, for example, once gave me a copy of a memorandum that hinted at an adulterous relationship between another DC official and a secretary. The relationship was common knowledge, however, and as far as I could tell, had no direct impact on daily routines. The only point of interest was that the data had been leaked to me at a specific time. Later on in the study, I was able to predict openings and reorganizations in the upper level of the hierarchy on the basis of such leaks alone. When two or three DC officials were in direct competition for a promotion, each contacted me with adverse information about the others.

How are data of this nature to be handled? Fortunately, there was no need to make a decision. In most cases, the data were irrelevant to the topic of study: parole outcomes. As a general rule, data given to me out of context were ignored for this reason alone. In the few cases where such data were relevant, they were ignored because they could not be corroborated.

This general principle was also applied to data obtained from POs. When a PO "fed" me a dossier, for example, I assumed that it was not representative of the other dossiers in his possession. In most cases, these data turned out to be more interesting to the PO than to me, that is, the data were irrelevant. In other cases, assertions made in the dossier could not be corroborated. The converse of this is true also. When a PO gave me unrestricted access to his files, I had some confidence in any data the PO "fed" me.

Finally, in at least two cases, DC officials granted interviews because they had resigned or had been fired. In such cases, it is natural to assume that the departing administrator has an ax to grind. This motive is suspect for an obvious reason. However, the interviews were regarded primarily as corroborative. Except for a few minor instances, they were not treated as data per se.

Corroboration. To ensure validity, data were corroborated whenever the opportunity presented itself. This usually amounted to checking items with other actors or with records. In many instances, for example, actors alleged that a superior had violated an ethical or legal code. Whereas I could not easily approach the superior for corroboration, I was often able to find some indirect evidence, pro or con, in the routine records. These˙ include dossiers, memoranda, vouchers, and payroll records. At one point in the study, I worked from a priority list. When I came across an item in my notes that seemed to require corroboration, I added the item to the list. I generally made no ad hoc immediate checks because, first, most of the items to be corroborated were not timely, and second, because ad hoc checks tend to draw notice.

The most obvious need for corroboration was the case where one actor made an assertion about another actor. These data were always corroborated or discarded. Another need for cor-roboration arose when I began to notice discrepancies in data. As my understanding of the routine situation grew throughout the study, I gave greater weight to data collected during the second and third phases a priori. When these data appeared to contradict data collected earlier, however, I returned to the source. Discrepancies were ordinarily due to misunderstandings on my part and all were cleared up by the end of the study.

Numbers. In *The Dynamics of a Bureaucracy,* Peter Blau uses both "soft" qualitative and "hard" quantitative data to support his arguments. There is an intuitive appeal to this double-edged approach. Qualitative data are best used to generate working hypotheses. Quantitative data are best used to test the hypoth-eses. The ideal research agenda will follow a conscious gener-ate/test/modify sequence iteratively, and in the long run, the strengths of one data type will control the weaknesses of the other. Now at no time in the course of this study did I ignore or discard available quantitative data. However, each of my attempts to collect "crucial" quantitative data failed.

The problems in this area are best illustrated by my attempts to measure report writing behaviors. While working on Chapter 5 (*Paperwork*), it occurred to me that I could test a number of hypotheses simply by measuring the *quantity* of writing done under certain conditions. This seemed to be a simple task when conceived but later proved to be nearly impossible.

I first tried measuring the amount of time POs spent on paperwork in the office. I discovered what I already knew, however: That POs spend little or no time in the office writing reports. Most of this work is done at home. Office time is spent answering phones, interviewing clients, and socializing with office-mates and supervisors.

I next considered going into the files in each office and simply counting the number of pages in each dossier. This figure could then be correlated with the predicted aspects of each case. Given the volume of records in each office, however, there was no way I could do this unnoticed.

I settled finally on "use of the Xerox machine" as the best quantitative indicator. Certain types of reports are always copied. Furthermore, the Xerox machines in each office have accounting sheets which each user must sign. It was a simple matter to copy these sheets and then code them as data. This method was both unobtrusive and precise.

After a few weeks, I knew how much Xeroxing each PO in every branch office had done. I then attempted a simple statistical analysis, with "use of the Xerox machine" as my dependent variable. The analysis failed to confirm my theories, however. The independent variables that I believed would predict how much report writing each PO would do all proved statistically insignificant.

At that point, I had two options. I could discard or modify my theories about report writing or I could discredit my quantitative indicators. I was reluctant to discard my theories because, first, I "knew" they were correct, and second, they were based on a common-sense notion of human nature. The second alternative, discrediting my quantitative indicators, was more attractive. According to Cook and Campbell (1975), a threat to construct validity occurs whenever there is a discrepancy between the construct variable and its operationalization. In this case, I searched for a discrepancy between the "amount of report writing" and "use of the Xerox machine," its operationalization.

I knew that Xerox copying was an imprecise measure of report writing because supervisors, POs, and secretaries make personal use of the Xerox machine. I had thought that the personal use was minimal, however. To investigate this assumption, I observed the Xerox machines in a few branch offices for an entire day. I discovered that many of the POs who were also full-time students copied books, journal articles, and class assignments on the office Xerox machines. In one branch office, over 80 percent of the copying done during my observation period was for personal use.

I admit to some pleasure at making this discovery. Had I not been able to discredit this quantitative indicator, I would have been forced to discard a number of theories. The displeasure in this would have come about simply because I "knew" the theories were correct.

"Knowing" and quantitative data come together when one "proves" the other. I have collected quantitative data only to the extent of simple counting: cases, incidents, and actors. These data cannot be analyzed statistically because they have no *variance* benchmark for comparison. In the end, the only "proof" of the argument I will present is its simplicity and commonsense nature. In the final chapter, I demonstrate how my argument fits into broader theories of how people behave. While this does not constitute "proof," it demonstrates that my theory of parole outcomes is reasonable. That is a type of "proof" in and of itself.

An Outline

My argument is that the men released from prison suffer outcomes that can be understood only in terms of a bureaucratic dynamic, a "black box" process. I suspect that no reasonable social scientist would question this. What might be questionable is the nature of this process. Traditional sociologies of parole have seen the process as being impersonal, at least for the largest part. My view, in contrast, sees the process as being a reflection of the interests at play in the parole agency. The notion of an impersonal, disinterested bureaucracy stems from the writings of Max Weber. The Weberian ideal-type of bureaucracy is a machine in the sense that it pursues a single-minded goal, performing routine tasks in an impersonal manner. The data show that this is not true for the largest part.

Each of the remaining chapters can stand individually, and in fact, substantial parts of Chapters 3 and 5 have appeared in social science journals as articles. However, there is a logical progression from chapter to chapter and this progression is my argument.

In Chapter 2 (*Power and Authority*), I describe the bureaucratic hierarchy of the DC. Groups of actors are defined as classes on the basis of a common interest. Power is not distributed up and down the hierarchy as authority. Parole officers, for example, are sometimes more powerful than high agency officials. Power is defined as the ability of a class to further its own interests, and in this sense, power is vested in the group. By far the most powerful group is the branch office team. The team consists of the supervisor and parole officers working out of one branch office. Each office has specific interests and the power to realize those interests.

In Chapter 3 (*Discretion*), I examine the power of individual parole officers in individual cases. There has been much attention paid to the discretion underlying parole revocation. However, the data I present show that discretion is more of an appearance than reality. While parole officers exercise gross discretionary power in theory, the actual exercise of power is constrained by structural variables. Structural constraints define the interests of the parole agency administrators. Administrators protect their interests through a number of mechanisms which, in effect, rob the individual parole officers of their discretionary power.

Chapters 2 and 3 describe the bureaucratic dynamic, or status quo. The interests of the branch office teams coincide to a certain extent with the interests of the central administration. In general, both groups avoid trouble. Each group defines trouble in a different way but recognizes that trouble for one group means trouble for the other. This recognition is the basis of the status quo. Overall, the bureaucracy favors those parole outcomes which leave the status quo unaffected.

In Chapter 4 (*Parolee-Types*), I describe the types of parolees who can make trouble. Parole officers diagnose new parolees, testing the feasibility of possible typing decisions. The typing decision addresses the parolee's potential for making trouble or for disrupting the bureaucratic dynamic. By applying the correct label to a new parolee, the parole officer can accommodate many routine problems. In other words, the parole officer can avoid trouble by making a correct typing decision.

In Chapter 5 (*Paperwork*), I describe how parole officers use records. As with the typing decision, records are used to avoid trouble or to maintain the status quo. Parole records then do not reflect the outcome-specific behavior of parolees, but rather, reflect the many routine problems which confront the parole officer.

Chapters 4 and 5 describe the role of the bureaucratic dynamic in the outcome process. For the most part, outcome will be determined by the initial typing decision. Moreover, each outcome requires a specific set of records. But because typing decisions and record-keeping address operational problems, that is, routine work-related problems and not necessarily parolee behavior, outcome is largely a function of the interests represented in the status quo. Put simply, like the rest of us, parole officers are interested in doing as little work as possible. Agency administrators are interested in avoiding political confrontations with other criminal justice bureaucracies. A given parole outcome becomes more likely or probable when it is consistent with these interests, that is, when it maintains the status quo.

In Chapter 6 (*A Sociology of Parole*), I explain the long-term process which supports the status quo. The parole bureaucracy recruits employees who have no interest in the status quo. In a sense, these uncommitted new employees must "become" parole officers. The socialization process requires that the new employee give up his personal values and accept the values defined in the status quo. Relating this phenomenon and the phenomena described in earlier chapters to studies of a public aid agency, I arrive at a minimal theory of the self-interested, self-generating bureaucracy. If there is one, the punch line is this: To understand the outcomes of social service cases, we must understand the motives and personal interests of the workers employed by social service agencies.

Chapter 2

POWER AND AUTHORITY

This chapter describes the working relationships and inter-actions among the three main groups of bureaucratic actors, DC officials, branch office supervisors, and POs. As shown in Figure 2.1, the authority structure of the DC is an unambiguous line hierarchy in which each level of authority is subordinated directly or indirectly to the highest level. POs are "line" em-ployees, situated at the very lowest level of the hierarchy.[1]

Except in the most superficial sense, the relationships among these three groups of actors cannot be analyzed strictly in terms of authority. For example, DC officials are entitled by statute to set policy, but in many cases, these officials lack the power to enforce a policy. Branch office supervisors, on the other hand, enjoy little authority but often exercise a great deal of power. Unlike authority, power is not always distributed in an unambiguous line from top to bottom. And whereas authority is vested in an office, power may accrue personally to the officeholder.[2]

In most cases, policy changes formulated at the bureaucracy's highest level will not affect the daily routine in the branch

Figure 2.1: An organizational chart of the bureaucracy. Five to nine POs will work under one supervisor in a branch office. All actors above the rank of supervisor are referred to as DC officials.

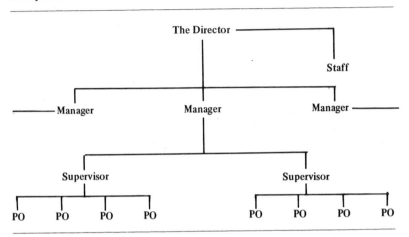

offices. Where there is some minimal effect, the branch office supervisor or even the POs themselves may reinterpret the policy change in a way that guarantees the status quo. But when the effect is profound and disruptive, supervisors and POs may actually rebel against the policy change. Bureaucratic rebellions move to zero-sum ends, so a successful rebellion requires a surrender of legitimate authority by the highest levels of the hierarchy. That DC officials will permit subordinates to usurp authority, suggests that DC officials have a stake in the status quo.

A successful rebellion will be analyzed here. As bureaucratic rebellions (and presumably, the necessary and sufficient conditions) are rare, however, there is no assurance that this is a "typical" rebellion. Nevertheless, an analysis of this episode provides an insight into the curious relationships among the three groups of actors.

DC Officials

Any DC employee above the rank of supervisor in Figure 2.1 will be called a "DC official." This category includes both the line managers and staff and the support staff. This latter group of DC officials ordinarily claims some technical skill and would include, for example, planners, purchasers, or personnel managers. The common denominator of these two types of DC official is their access to debates on policy alternatives. While a systems analyst might have little direct interest in many matters of policy, he would at least be present at meetings where these matters are debated.[3] Branch office supervisors and POs, in contrast, never have a direct knowledge of these debates, but rather, learn of them second-hand.

DC officials are remarkably homogeneous in terms of background. Most have formal credentials and experience in management and most entered the organization laterally. Few if any "started at the bottom" of the DC and worked their way upwards. This factor may account for the striking difference in attitude between DC officials and their subordinates in the field. A DC official who has a degree in administration, for example, expressed this opinion: "The DC is a business. The problems and solutions are the same. Our customer is the public and our product is parolees. Most POs don't care enough about the customer and certainly not enough about product quality."

DC officials view themselves as scientific decision-makers, and in this role, general managerial skills are more valuable than specific knowledge. POs hold a nearly opposite view on this point. Speaking of one DC official, for example, a PO complained: "He's a know-it-all desk jockey. I've got a college degree too but it's not worth anything. I learned everything I know about being a PO out there on the streets. That's where you learn what the DC is all about."

Regardless of educational attainment, POs place a great value on this so-called "street" wisdom. DC officials, who are ignorant in this respect, are often thought to be lacking in the types of knowledge required for making decisions that affect the street level. When a policy change affects the street level status quo, POs are likely to challenge the policy on the grounds that it lacks "street" wisdom.

In 1974, it was decided at the very highest levels of the DC that POs should no longer carry firearms.[4] POs resented this new policy because, first, it violated a traditional "right," and second, because the policy had been formulated in ignorance. Addressing a group of POs, one DC official described the official reasoning this way: "We're struggling to build a modern professional image and gun-toting POs are not consistent with that image. We want parole *counselors,* not POs. If you think you can't perform your duties without a gun, then there's no room for you in the DC." While agreeing with this reasoning in principle, POs felt that the practical, street-level considerations had not been weighed. Moreover, most POs saw a more cynical motive in the policy change: "They're overreacting to some bad publicity. They want us to risk our lives now just so they can get good press clippings."

The basis of the conflict then was not only general versus "street" wisdom, but also, motive. POs often accuse DC officials of stressing publicity concerns at the expense of "professional" concerns. Regarding the wisdom of the policy, both sides saw the other as being incompetent to decide the matter. One PO summed up the consensus: "I think the big wheels know what's best in the abstract but when it comes to actually getting things done, they don't know anything. I'm the one who has to go out on the streets at night, so I'm the only one who knows whether I need a gun."

The distinction between power and authority came sharply into focus. The branch office supervisors, who are charged with enforcing policy at the street level, sided with their POs. No supervisor enforced the policy; all signed a petition that the POs had circulated. In one branch office, the supervisor was reprimanded by his superiors. As this supervisor related the incident:

> I just acted humble and told him that as far as I knew, no PO in my office was carrying a gun. That's the truth too—as far as I know, haha. Then I told him that he could come down here every morning and frisk my POs. I'm sure not going to do that. My job is to report any infractions that I know about, and as far as I know, none of my POs is carrying a gun.

But in fact, POs were openly and deliberately flaunting their defiance of the policy. Whereas POs might have previously attempted to conceal their pistols, many were now wearing ostentatious external holster apparatuses. It appeared also that DC officials were staying away from the branch offices in order to avoid a direct confrontation on the issue.[5] One DC official confirmed this suspicion: "Mr. Chaseham wants no confrontations. He feels that the supervisors can handle the situation if they're given enough time. The revolt will die of boredom. Enforcing regulations in an organization of this size and complexity is not an easy thing."

In the third month of the rebellion, a PO was arrested for carrying a pistol. The prosecutor turned the case over to the DC for administrative action, and under these circumstances, the DC was forced to take official notice. A disciplinary proceeding was instituted against the PO. Other POs began to collect donations for legal fees and the case became a rallying point. POs who were asked to predict the outcome of this case invariably answered: "We'll win. We'll take this to the Supreme Court and it'll be front page news all the way there. They can't afford the publicity so they'll have to back down." This prediction proved correct. The offending PO was given a nominal reprimand. A few days later, the no-firearms policy was amended. Thereafter, POs were allowed to carry firearms, but only revolvers (no semiautomatic pistols), only while on duty, and only after completing an accredited pistol safety course. For all practical purposes, the rebellion had succeeded. More than one DC official interpreted this outcome differently, however: "I don't think it's fair to say that we 'caved in.' It was simply a matter of refining the policy. Our only concern was in the safety of the POs. We wanted to eliminate a potential cause of serious accidents. Once we made that clear, the field personnel were happy to comply with the regulations." This episode illustrates the power dynamics of the bureaucracy. DC officials enjoy the legitimate authority to set policy. Due to the nature of the organization, however, DC officials lack the absolute power required to enforce a policy.

The Supervisors

During the height of the firearms rebellion, a branch office supervisor told me:

> If they'd let us in on it, we'd have handled it without stirring up a hornet's nest. Some POs don't need guns and some of the POs who *do* need guns shouldn't be permitted to carry them. But that's for the supervisor to decide. I'll tell you another thing. I know how to make a rule like that stick because I know what makes my POs tick. But I'm not going to enforce any rule that bypasses my good judgment or that undermines my authority in this office.

This was a typical attitude. On this point, it is revealing to examine the motives of the supervisors in this episode. One supervisor summed it up this way: "Do you know what would happen if I enforced that (no-firearms) rule? My POs would be afraid to go out in the streets and they'd start faking their reports—which makes more work for me. They do enough of that now anyway. Believe me, if I enforced that rule, my work here would triple." So the supervisors had a personal stake in the firearms rebellion. Had they enforced the edict, their workloads would have increased dramatically.

The supervisors see their position in the organization as midway between labor (the POs) and management (DC officials), with responsibilities to both but also with certain traditional rights that neither group can challenge. The supervisors' duties consist primarily of managing the branch offices. These duties often amount to simple bookkeeping chores, such as making sure that monthly reports are filed on time, but the duties also include, implicitly at least, *interpreting* policies. A supervisor does not ordinarily enforce DC policies, but rather, enforces his interpretation of the policies. Within this context, DC officials and POs have certain expectations of the supervisor. First, consider this typical statement made by a DC official:

> The supervisors are our "noncoms." A PO can lie to me but he can't lie to his supervisor because his supervisor was a PO himself at one

time. We give our supervisors a wide latitude in running their offices. That's because they know the nuts-and-bolts issues better than we do. We tell them what we want done and they get it done. We may not always agree with their methods but they're effective and that's what counts.

Then consider this typical statement made by a PO: "Terry's main job as I see it is protecting us from the higher-ups. The average DC administrator is a political hack. Terry's job is to keep the hacks away from us." To the administrators then, supervisors serve the function of curbing the wild excesses and demands of headstrong young POs. As long as the supervisors are effective in this respect, the administrators are willing to permit each supervisor wide latitude in interpreting DC policy. In contrast, POs see their supervisors serving the function of tempering the unrealistic demands of the administrators. As long as the supervisor is effective in this respect, he commands an intense personal loyalty from his POs.[6] This loyalty is apparent in the everyday speech and behavior of POs. For example: "Terry (our supervisor) looks out for us and we look out for him. Sometimes I get frustrated with things but I try not to do anything that would cause trouble for Terry. He's been pretty good to me, pretty liberal, and I don't want to do anything that would hurt him." However, supervisors have an advantage so far as dealings with their POs are concerned. One supervisor admitted: "I agree that I'm well liked by my POs but there's a reason for that. When I have to put my foot down, the POs think I'm doing it because my superiors ordered me to do it. When I let them get away with something, it's because I'm a nice guy. That's a good position to be in because my POs will do just about anything I ask." It is apparent then that supervisors are in the position of serving two masters, and because both are served well, supervisors enjoy power.

A second source of power comes from the common backgrounds of the supervisors. Unlike DC officials or POs, the supervisors have extensive experience in other social service bureaucracies. During their first careers, before joining the DC, the supervisors built reputations as bureaucratic loyalists. This is an important factor in the unofficial scheme of things. As one DC official remarked: "We have an outstanding group of supervisors. All of them worked in other agencies. The value of that, as I see it, is that they've been molded into loyalists. Whatever one of the supervisors does, no matter how strange it seems, I know that the best interests of the DC are being served. They always think of the organization first." But there is a more important factor:

> "It's no secret why we made Matt a supervisor in that office. We were getting a lot of flack from the prosecutor and Matt spent twenty-two years in the prosecutor's office. When we promoted him to supervisor, we neutralized the prosecutor. Whenever we have a problem with the prosecutor, we let Matt handle it informally."[7]

The bureaucratic loyalty factor explains why DC officials permit the supervisors to run their offices with great discretion: "Sometimes we don't understand why a supervisor is doing something but we assume that it's for the good of the DC." The neutralization factor is interpreted similarly. The DC routinely deals with other criminal justice bureaucracies, so having an "insider" in a supervisory position facilitates a smooth political interaction with other agencies.[8]

A third and final source of power for the supervisor is the special knowledge, or the appearance of special knowledge at least, that is associated with his midway position in the organization. POs, for example, believe that, unlike themselves, their supervisors understand the arcane workings of the DC: "Sometimes I don't understand why Terry has me do something but I always assume that there's a good reason. He knows what's going on downtown and I don't. That kind of inside knowledge is important in this job. If you get along with your supervisor, he'll pull your coat to a lot of inside things."

DC officials, on the other hand, believe that the supervisors understand the "nuts and bolts" of parole work, and more importantly, the "mentality" of the street-level bureaucrat. Needless to say, DC officials are ignorant in this area of knowledge: "Terry is an intelligence source, I suppose. He has his ear to the ground and anticipates trouble. I'm removed from the source, so I have to trust his judgment in those things. I'm inclined to believe him when he tells me something because he's familiar with his districts."

At this point, the matter of performance must be considered. Above all, a supervisor is powerful because he performs favorably with respect to the interested parties. One supervisor acknowledged this factor explicitly:

> Chaseham lets us (supervisors) get away with murder because he doesn't have any choice. If he tried to run this office from downtown, my POs would beat him to death with problems. Besides, I deliver and Chaseham knows it. He sees very little trouble coming out of this office. Oh, he could get rid of me if he wanted to—but he doesn't want to. I deliver and as long as I keep on delivering, he lets me pretty much alone.

The three sources of power discussed here need not be distinct, and in fact, it would be difficult to assess their separate relative weights. What is certain, however, is that the supervisors *are* powerful and that this power is tolerated because, as the other interested parties see it, the supervisors "deliver." This may mean, on one hand, that the supervisors are able to control the misguided behavior of rash young POs. On the other hand, it may mean that the supervisors are able to blunt the unrealistic and "unprofessional" demands of DC administrators.

Returning now to the firearms rebellion, it is apparent that the supervisors "delivered," at least as far as POs were concerned. This can be contrasted with Weber's notion of charismatic authority which, according to Gert and Mills (1958: 249), requires that, "The charismatic leader gains and maintains authority solely by proving his strength in life. If he wants to be a prophet, he must perform miracles; if he wants to be a war lord, he must perform heroic deeds." And if he wants to be a supervisor, he must "deliver." To DC officials, of course, the performance of the supervisors in the firearms rebellion appeared to be a betrayal of trust. Many DC officials had expected the supervisors to quell the uprising in their own way, and thus, had taken no decisive action against the rebels. That this betrayal was tolerated, suggests that the supervisors "deliver" more important things in the long run.

In their own branch offices, the supervisors enjoy supreme authority. I happened to be sitting in an office one day when a supervisor received a phone call from his immediate superior. The only purpose of the call was to announce that the office would be visited by a group of DC officials that day. *This was more than a warning.* Over a period of months, I noticed that DC officials never entered the branch offices without first phoning ahead. This traditional understanding between DC officials and supervisors typifies the power of the supervisor in his own office.

The supervisors themselves are conscious of their power. If nothing else, they cite it as a major source of job satisfaction: "I don't think I'd enjoy my job if the shots were being called from downtown. I'm like the captain of a ship, I guess. The admirals decide where the fleet is going, but on my ship, I'm the boss." This simile is apt. For the supervisor, power consists of nearly total discretion within his branch office: "It's understood that I can organize and run my office the way I see fit. That's why every branch office is different. They're all like separate little kingdoms." And as will be demonstrated here, the power of the supervisors is an important component in the operation of the bureaucracy.

Power, or control of the branch offices, is manifested in a number of concrete facets. The two most important ways, however, might be control of intraoffice promotions and arbitrary control of work standards. First, while the DC has a well defined system of pay increments,[9] there are a number of intraoffice job changes that amount to promotions for the POs. These noncivil service (and hence, unofficial) promotions are controlled absolutely by the branch office supervisors. Examples of these jobs are the "trainer," who is responsible for breaking in new POs; the "specialists" or "liaison" POs, who work with special types of parolees only or who co-ordinate the branch office's dealings with special programs and outside agencies; and the "acting supervisor" or "second man," who is second in command of the branch office.

POs value these promotions for a number of reasons, usually centered around prestige, easier duties, and personal interests. Supervisors use these promotions to reward deserving POs but there will ordinarily be other pragmatic considerations in the promotion. During the course of this study, a "trainer" position opened up in one of the branch offices. One PO in particular felt that he was most deserving of the job because, "I've been in this office longer than any other PO. I know more about the districts and more about the daily operations than any other PO. I'm the logical choice." But the supervisor designated a PO from another branch office as the "trainer." There was some initial displeasure among the POs over this decision but all agreed that their supervisor could, if he wished, give the job to an outsider. At a staff meeting held about a week after the announcement, the supervisor said: "As you know, I'm letting Whitney, who works out of the [other] office do our training. I've got a reason for doing it that way but I can't go into it right now."[10]

The POs who attended this meeting seemed to accept this. None complained or asked further questions. About a month later, I questioned the supervisor about the affair. He told me:

Frank did deserve the promotion but I couldn't give it to him. That was a hard decision for me to make. What I'm going to do is write Frank up for a civil service merit promotion. He probably won't get it but it'll be a public pat on the back for him. . . . Frank just isn't smart enough to be my trainer. I don't mean that Frank isn't intelligent because he is. When I say smart, I mean that there's a smart way to do everything. Maybe it's not the right way, maybe it's even the wrong way, but it's the way that causes me the least trouble. Well, Frank just doesn't do things the smart way. He never has.

But why not tell Frank the situation? Given his intelligence, he could no doubt become smart if he saw an incentive:

I'd feel funny discussing that, and knowing Frank, he'd probably get indignant. Believe it or not, Frank is the only PO in (named county) who never broke a rule. That's not smart. Being smart is like having an attitude problem. You get smarter as you grow older but there's got to be something there to start with. Frank won't get smarter no matter how long he's on the job.

Only smart POs are given intraoffice promotions and for the obvious reason:

A smart PO like Whitney will show a new man the smart way to do things. Also, Whitney will tell me if he thinks a new man won't work out. I can't put myself in a position where I'm telling a new man to break rules. New men serve six-month probationary periods before they get into civil service. I might have to fire a new man at the end of his six months and I don't want any new man to say that I ordered him to break DC rules and then fired him when he wouldn't. POs have very political jobs. They have to compromise and that means bending rules—which isn't the same as breaking them. I expect my POs to do that, but if I find out about it, I have to discipline the PO. Ha-ha-ha. It's funny. My biggest problem is teaching POs how to pull something over on me. That's funny, isn't it?

This attitude is pervasive. Consider a related statement by a PO:

Each case is different, so you can't have a set of inflexible rules. Terry wants us to do certain things in certain ways but he can't come right out and tell us that. He never tells you that you did something the wrong way either. He just hands the case back to you and asks you to do some more work on it. Usually, I think about the case and see what's wrong with it, but if I don't, I ask Whitney. . . . No, you can't go by the book because they don't print those things up. You have to pretend you're doing everything by the book, though.

The charade revealed by this episode and comment is one of the most important social interactions between the supervisor and his POs. The following anecdote, related to me by a supervisor, describes the interaction from a particular functional perspective:

When Joe first starts working in this office, he comes in here with a monthly report for me to sign. "Matt," he says to me, "this is the best parolee I've ever had. He's going to make it with no trouble." You know how POs sometimes get enthusiastic about a parolee, right? Well, I read the report over and says to him, "You must be mistaken, Joe. The parolee you're writing about in this report isn't going to make it. He's going to be back in the joint within ninety days." I hands the report back to him and he walks out of here. The next day he comes back in with the report rewritten and hands it to me. I look it over and says to him, "You're the best PO I have, Joe. Why, you've rehabilitated this man in less than twenty-four hours. It's a miracle!" Well, of course, it wasn't that Joe had rehabilitated the man, it was that Joe had learned how to write reports. Naturally, I'd have kept giving the report back to him until he'd done it right.

Branch office supervisors transmit information to their POs through a trial-and-error charade. Supervisors use their traditional right to control intraoffice promotions to place smart POs in key positions. From these key positions, smart POs can advise their peers from a position of authority. Supervisors use their traditional right to set quality standards to discourage undesired forms of behavior: "If one of my POs makes trouble for me, I make trouble for him by forcing him to do extra work. That's easy, you know, because in this office, I'm the one who decides when a PO has put enough time into an investigation or into a report."

Power then, as manifested in the control of intra-office promotions and the control of work standards, is used by the supervisors to run their offices in an efficient and trouble-free manner.

WHY SUPERVISORS USE THEIR POWER

As the general topic of "trouble" has been raised, it can be reasonably stated that supervisors use their power to avoid trouble. Supervisors cite many potential sources of trouble and this will vary from office to office. However, both *nonconformity* and *ambiguity* illustrate the general concepts and underlying circumstances.

As a rule, supervisors want their POs to submit uniform reports. A new PO in one of the branch offices often wrote lengthy site investigation reports. The other POs in the office disapproved of this, and from time to time, would make jokes at the nonconformist's expense. The jokes were meant to be a norm-enforcing mechanism, but as the new PO was not aware of the norm for site investigation reports, the jokes were interpreted as a personal attack:

> Whitney called me "Sally Social Worker." I don't think that's funny and I don't think he means it as a joke either. He only says it when the other fellows are around. I'm just trying to fit in here. . . . My site investigation reports do have something to do with it but I don't think that it's anybody's business. I'm not saying that anybody has to do it my way. I just happen to think that the site investigation is the most important part of this job. It's a free country, though, and if other people have a different opinion, that's their right. I don't tell them how to do their work and I don't want them telling me how to do mine.[11]

But the norm-breaking PO was wrong on this point. No matter how complete one of his site investigation reports was, his supervisor handed it back to him for more work. After a month of this treatment, he said:

> I don't get it. I do the best site reports in this office and I get the most shit. Did you ever see one of Whitney's reports? He never writes more than a half-page and Matt never sends one back to him for more work. Obviously, anytime you say something substantial, you raise questions. Matt never rejects Whitney's reports because Whitney never says anything substantial. Matt's rewarding people for doing sloppy work whether he realizes it or not.

When it became apparent to the new PO that it would take him weeks to complete a site investigation report that otherwise should have taken no more than an hour, he began to compromise his ideals. The jokes stopped, and within a few weeks, the norm-breaker had become "one of the fellows."

The supervisor's method of norm enforcement, making the nonconformist work harder, is more effective than group ridicule, the method used by POs themselves. When the supervisor's motives are understood, however, an important point is revealed. In this case, the supervisor explained: "I want all the site investigation reports going out of this office to be the same length. If I let a five-page report get out of here, the people downtown are going to ask me why all my POs aren't writing five-page reports. That's the way the people downtown think."

This is why POs set work norms for their peers: a "rate buster" will cause the minimum work standards to be raised. The supervisor has no direct interest in this matter, however. His motive for enforcing the norm is personal:

> I have only two interests in the site investigation report. I want to make sure there's nothing in it that could come back to haunt me in the future, so if the report is brief, I won't have any trouble with it. If it's not brief, I have to go over it carefully. When a site report gets to be five pages long, I'm going to have to spend a week checking it over and usually I'm going to have to send it back to the PO to clarify things. Now that gets into my second interest. I have maybe two hundred site reports cross my desk in a year and I'm working under a deadline on each one of them. A site investigation is supposed to give the PO an opportunity to see the parolee's home environment and that's important. But the report itself isn't. I have only one rule for those reports: keep 'em simple.

Supervisors also abhor *ambiguity* and for similar reasons. POs must write monthly reports on their parolees. The supervisor will ordinarily countersign the monthly reports without comment. Should a report contain an ambiguous element, however, the supervisor will return it to the PO with a request for more work on the case. When this happens, the PO has two practical options. He may do the further work as requested or he may rewrite the report. The latter option is often the easier of the two. In one case, a PO who had been working in a branch office for less than a year had a monthly report returned to him with instructions to file a revocation warrant against the parolee. The

PO told me: "Terry wants me to go after a revocation warrant
on this. I don't know what he means. This isn't strong enough
for a warrant. They'd throw it out in hearing. I guess it's
something that I'd be better off not even mentioning in the
report."

The PO rewrote the report, leaving out the incident he had
originally reported. This time, the supervisor signed the report
perfunctorily. What the PO learned from this episode was to
eschew ambiguity in his monthly reports. The supervisor's motives in this respect are:

> What I'm doing when I okay those reports is checking to see if a
> report requires some sort of official action. When you look at it that
> way, you can see that there are only two kinds of reports. To get
> past me, a report has to be either one kind or the other. It can't be
> somewhere in between. If I let a wishy-washy report get past me,
> then maybe a year from now, somebody in the DC is going to ask
> me why I didn't take some action on the case. I want a monthly
> report to say either that the guy is a model parolee or else that he's a
> menace. . . . When I told Phil to go after a warrant in that case, I was
> being sarcastic. I wouldn't have okayed a warrant for [that offense].
> But Phil got the message. If you can't go after a warrant or at least
> give the parolee a warning, don't report the incident.

In this situation, POs themselves have only a minimal interest in
the work norm. POs would probably not bring group sanctions
against a peer who wrote ambiguous monthly reports because
POs do not see ambiguity as a direct threat. Supervisors on the
other hand have a concrete interest in this area.

The POs

As few as five or as many as nine POs work out of one branch
office. As the branch offices are separated geographically, and
as each office is run by a powerful supervisor, styles of work,
attitudes, and social characteristics of POs vary widely. In some
respects, however, all POs are the same. This is particularly true
with respect to certain work norms that, to the POs, amount to

traditional "rights." Before examining these rights, the concept of legitimation by tradition must be discussed. According to POs, certain rights are legitimate because they have "always" existed. While granting this, there is no ready explanation as to why some rights survive and others do not. One plausible hypothesis is that all such rights have a functional utility to the bureaucracy, but that if a certain right loses its utility over time, it will fall by the wayside. Other rights will survive and become part of the bureaucracy's tradition. Of course, the notion of bureaucratic inertia must be considered. Once a right has been incorporated into the traditions of a bureaucracy, it necessarily dies slowly, but it dies nevertheless.

Now, as might be expected, traditions themselves vary from office to office. But in *all* offices, there are two unquestioned traditions. These are, first, the sanctity of the case, and second, the sanctity of territory.

First, the case is the basic work-unit of the PO, and in any given case, a PO expects no interference from his peers. The normal attitude of POs towards this right is best illustrated by the following example. A PO once told me:

> One of my former parolees called me today with a complaint about Jerry. I think Jerry made a bad decision in that case. . . . I told Jerry I got the call but I didn't mention my opinion. There's an unwritten rule that you don't interfere with another PO's cases. . . . The man was probably exaggerating. Anyway, if things are as bad as he claims, he can get rid of Jerry. All he has to do is move into another parole district. All parolees know that. And if he did move into my district, Jerry wouldn't interfere with me, so I'm not going to interfere with him. I didn't encourage the man to move into my district. I was annoyed that he called me and I let him know it. See, you can't side openly with a parolee against one of your partners. That's like a courtesy or a rule of etiquette.

I have observed a number of cases where parolees moved from one district to another merely to change POs. POs themselves accept these moves and do not ordinarily react against the mover.[12] In one such case, a PO commented:

I'm not offended at all. That's not the first time it's happened and it won't be the last. I've had parolees move *into* my district just so they could have me for their PO. It's just a matter of different strokes for different folks. Usually it's a psychological thing for the parolee *and* the PO. Both of 'em feel uncomfortable with the other, so the parolee moves and both of 'em are better off.

This aspect of the PO-parolee interaction often serves as a moral rationalization for the PO: "If he doesn't like the way I handled that, he can move."

The PO's peers may be interested in a given case because the PO's decision may have offended their sense of morality. During the course of this study, a number of POs criticized the behavior of a peer.[13] Absolute noninterference is the norm, however, and it is enforced by the branch office supervisor who, himself, will not ordinarily interfere with a PO. This statement is typical:

Occasionally I call a PO in here to discuss a case but that's not interference. My only interest is that, no matter what the PO does, he protects himself. Otherwise I don't interfere. I was a PO once and I know that POs like to make their own decisions. That's a big morale factor. I'm only interested in getting the cases processed and I don't care how a PO does that as long as he protects himself.

Supervisors invariably cite "morale" as a motive for not interfering in the case decisions of their POs.

Noninterference by peers is another matter. POs ordinarily try to enforce work norms by means of group disapproval and ridicule, but as noted earlier, this method is often ineffective. There are several reasons for this. First, POs interact with peers for no more than eight hours per week, as opposed to an assembly line, say, where workers interact with peers for eight hours per day, five days per week. Second, POs view themselves as professional workers, bound by internalized codes. Given this factor, a norm-breaking PO can easily rationalize away any group sanction: "They're just behaving unprofessionally." It is important to note, however, that POs will *not* openly criticize a peer for a case decision. In the earlier episode, the norm-breaking PO was ridiculed for the *length* of his reports, not for their content. Noninterference in the case decision is in fact the norm and it is enforced by the branch office supervisor. In the few cases I observed, the offending PO was counseled by his supervisor, and realizing the consequences, never again interfered with another PO's case decisions. The supervisor's motives in this area are obvious:

I won't stand for one of my POs second-guessing another. If I tolerated that, I'd have grudges going on here. Pretty soon I'd have an office full of snitches. A few years ago, I had a PO who couldn't keep his nose out of the other caseloads. I spoke to him about it but that didn't do any good. He thought he was the conscience of the DC if you know what I mean. Well, I finally got fed up with his meddling and I gave him a taste of his own medicine. I went over his files and found unfinished work for him to do. The sonofabitch quit about a month later and that was a good thing too because I was just getting warmed up.

POs usually defend the norm of noninterference in professional terms such as "client confidentiality." Yet the functional utility of the norm will explain its existence better. Noninterference enhances cooperation between the supervisor and his POs. The supervisor may require a PO to make unpopular case decisions, and given the noninterference norm, the PO can make the expedient decision without fearing for his reputation among his peers. Noninterference then ensures the orderly and efficient operation of the branch offices, and in this sense, has a definite functional utility to the bureaucracy.

Territoriality, the second traditional right of POs, has its roots in the political history of the bureaucracy. According to one veteran PO: "In the old days, these jobs went to ward heelers. You'd assign a PO to his home precinct because he knew the voters there. He could ring a few doorbells every day, keep up his contacts. That's why they set up the caseloads this way. I guess the reason why they never changed it is that everyone likes this setup."

It should be noted that few modern, urban parole bureaucracies still have rigidly defined, geographical caseload-districts.

The Federal parole bureaucracy, for example, randomly assigns parolees to caseloads regardless of the parolee's geographical residence. This method of assigning parolees to POs ensures that all caseloads will be roughly similar. No single caseload will be lopsided in terms of its relative size or distribution of parolees by characteristics. Recognizing the obvious advantages to this method, we must ask why the traditional caseload-districts still exist. The answer is that, as the veteran PO hypothesized, "everyone likes this setup."

Styles of work vary greatly from PO to PO. For example, some POs spread their fieldwork out evenly across the month while other POs crowd all their fieldwork into one or two days. Some POs make monthly "eyeball" contacts with their parolees while other POs rely heavily on phone and mail contacts. These differences are often personal choices that the POs have made to tailor their work schedules to outside interests.[14] POs never attribute differences in style to the individual, however, but rather, to the district. In one case, a PO took over a district that another PO had handled for nearly five years. The new PO immediately reorganized the monthly reporting schedule for the district. His explanation was: "This district's been changing for years. Bob's way of running it wasn't wrong. It's just that this is a different district than it was five years ago. Bob would have reorganized his schedule eventually and he would have done it the way I'm doing it now."

POs are assigned a territory and all parolees who reside within the territorial limits will be included in the PO's caseload. Once a PO has been assigned to a specific district, he can control the district in much the same way that a supervisor controls the branch office. The PO can selectively enforce rules and regulations within his caseload, for example, or he can devise a work style which permits moonlighting: "The difference between me and Bob on the subject of narcotics has nothing to do with our personal philosophies. Our districts are different. He *has* to tolerate a certain level of drug use in his district. I don't have that problem in my district."

Territorial rights are important to the PO because territoriality introduces an element of certainty and regularity into the job. If the PO enrolls in a graduate degree program, for example, he knows that his schedule will be constant over the next few semesters. Supervisors recognize this factor and treat it as a fringe benefit. During the course of this study, two geographically adjacent parole districts had lopsided caseloads, one large and one small. When I suggested to the supervisor that the caseload sizes be equalized by redefining the districts, he answered: "I won't fool around with district boundaries as a rule. A district actually *belongs* to a PO, and as long as he handles it properly, I won't touch it. I have one PO in this office who's worked the same district for eight years. I'd be creating morale problems if I fooled around with the map." And, in general, a PO can count on his territorial rights so long as he handles his territory without creating problems for the supervisor. Furthermore, the supervisor cannot ordinarily rearrange the district of one PO, say a PO who is unable to handle the district effectively, without also rearranging the districts of other POs. This further guarantees the sanctity of the district.

Territorial rights lead to a minor form of corruption, which should be noted at this point. If a PO's district generates an extremely small caseload for an extended period of time, the DC will change the boundaries of the district. POs therefore will attempt to "paper" their caseloads against any reductions in caseload size. One PO explained this phenomenon:

> The DC wants me to discharge parolees after they've served *about* eighteen months on parole. There's a little trick you can pull that inflates your caseload. If I make my parolees serve an average of three extra months—twenty-one months on parole, my caseload size goes up by twenty percent. I can do that just by relying on the red tape boys downtown too. That's the way I keep my caseload at a fairly constant size.[15]

These factors reinforce the geographic stability of the districts.

It is apparent here that the rigidly defined geographical districts give the PO some power. As one PO noted:

> Having your own district day after day gives you an advantage. I've had my district now for over two years and I know what's cooking

down there. Nobody else does. I know who the important cops are, who the community people are, and how to handle them. If they jerked me out of this district now, it'd take them a year to build those relationships back up. That gives me a lot of protection.

So understandably, the other parties of interest must derive some benefits from the arrangement. For supervisors, the advantages of territoriality can be explained largely as a function of branch office morale. In addition to this factor, however, the supervisors realize that territoriality enables the PO to better coordinate his work with other criminal justice agencies. With respect to the police department, for example:

A PO gets to know the sergeants in his district, so when trouble pops up, he straightens it out with them. It's easy to straighten a problem out when you know the people you're dealing with and when they know you. Otherwise what would happen is that the problem would get passed to me and I'd pass it on to the DC people downtown. Our bigshots would have to sit down with their bigshots and straighten the problem out. See? My POs handle a lot of problems with the police just by talking to sergeants and they can do that because they've been working in the same districts for a long time and know their counterparts on the police force.

This subject will be covered in more detail in the next chapter.

As far as DC officials are concerned, territoriality amounts to a useful punishment-reward system. As one DC official noted:

The districts aren't included in the civil service job descriptions, so in theory, we can transfer an incompetent PO down to the Blood Bucket. Most POs resign after six months in that district. There are also two or three relatively good districts—ninety percent white caseloads. We can use these as carrots. Good POs get good districts.

Given the power dynamics in the DC, however, the utility of the punishment-reward system is uncertain. A number of cases where POs were transferred as punishment were observed. In all of these cases, however, the transfer was endorsed by the PO's supervisors and peers. It seems unlikely that a DC official, no matter how great his authority, could unilaterally transfer a PO from a "good" to a "bad" district. Many administrators never-theless see transfers as a viable means of controlling trouble makers.[16]

There is another, more realistic advantage to having rigidly defined districts, however. In one case, a PO was involved in a major dispute with police officers over a parolee. A short time later, the PO was transferred to a much "better" district. Assuming that DC officials want to avoid disputes with other criminal justice agencies, it appears that the PO was rewarded for making trouble. A branch office supervisor easily explained the paradox:

> Harrison's one of the finest POs in [named county]. He wasn't at fault in that mess because he was following his supervisor's orders. But you have to be realistic too. There was a personality clash there between Harrison and the cop and something like that will cause trouble between the two organizations. What do we do about that, huh? We move Harrison to a district out in the suburbs. Harrison's happy, the cop's happy, and Harrison's new supervisor is happy because he's getting a damn good PO out of the deal.

Later in the conversation, the supervisor stated that the transfer was initiated by one of the highest officials in the DC. This assertion was backed up by the written memoranda that were available. It is apparent then that DC officials see territoriality as a means of optimizing the political interactions with other criminal justice agencies at the street level.

With respect to the sanctity of the case and the sanctity of territory, it is apparent that these traditional rights enhance the PO's work environment. What is not immediately apparent is that these rights also underly the PO's power. On this point, the statement of a branch office supervisor is most revealing:

> I have to depend on my POs a lot because they're in a position to know what's going on with their clients. Sure, I see the monthly reports but those don't tell me what I have to know. A smart PO puts as little as possible in writing. When I get an inquiry or a complaint, I have to ask the PO what to do. If there's nothing to worry about, he tells me that. If there is something to worry about,

he tells me that too. Most of my POs anticipate trouble before I hear about it and they give me an advance notice. That gives me a chance to work up a little protection. Let me tell you exactly the way it is. A PO can really stick it to his supervisor if he wants to. That's why the most important part of my job is getting along with my POs. I treat every one of my POs like family.

Other supervisors made similar statements, although not so explicit. At no time did any supervisor make a statement that was inconsistent with the meaning of this one. Just as POs realize the power held by their supervisors, the supervisors realize the power held by their POs. The efficient and trouble free operation of the branch offices rests on this mutual realization.

There is a general point to be made about power in the parole bureaucracy. First, authority per se subsumes power, and thus, DC officials are not powerless. Where they appear to be powerless, the value of special knowledge is seen. In the most general sense then, the power supervisors and POs have rests on their esoteric knowledge of the specific situation. Weber addresses this factor under the rubric of *secrecy,* which, according to Gerth and Mills (1958: 233), holds that, "Every bureaucracy seeks to increase the superiority of the professionally informed by keeping their knowledge and intentions secret." So the PO's power has its roots in his esoteric knowledge of a territory and of a caseload. Similarly, the supervisor's power lies in his esoteric knowledge of the branch office. Moreover, as the supervisors are chosen in a particular way, all supervisors have an esoteric knowledge of another criminal justice agency. That this special knowledge lends power to the supervisors, can be seen in the way POs and DC officials speak of it: supervisors are said to have "connections."

The branch office becomes a seat of power when the supervisor and his POs share, or exchange,[17] their knowledge. Each branch office is a clique then, or a coalition, in which the supervisor and his POs interact as a team in pursuit of common interests. This interest is ordinarily synonymous with the efficient and trouble-free operation of the branch office, for when an office operates in this way, interference from higher authorities is minimal. Needless to say, supervisors and POs share this interest.

Note finally that knowledge follows from the routine exercise of traditional rights, and to complete the dynamic, that the traditional rights are secured and maintained through a judicious but routine exercise of power.

THE "PROFESSIONALS" [18]

The separation of the branch offices by geography prevents any routine interaction among POs from different offices. As separation magnifies the differences among the various offices, and as this leads to secrecy within the offices, separation increases the power of each branch office team. However, this is gained at the cost of the power that POs might wield as a class if they were to interact with each other routinely. Where POs from different branch offices interact at all, usually after-hours and usually outside the offices, a well defined clique is seen. These are the "professionals."

Clique formation was preceded and caused to some extent by an abrupt change in hiring policies. In the last five years, a sudden influx of Federal anticrime monies has enabled (or forced) the DC to expand its field staff substantially. However, hiring guidelines attached to these monies have forced (or enabled) the DC to raise its minimum standards. POs hired before this time are often members of one political party and were given their jobs, or so most claim, as patronage. Few of these POs have any educational credentials related to their work; some do not have high school diplomas. Younger POs, in contrast, were hired under a strictly enforced civil service code and usually have undergraduate degrees in a social science or in social work; some have graduate degrees.[19] These younger POs are largely clique members or sympathizers.

The evidence for the existence of a clique consists mainly of observed patterns of after-hours socializing. As most of the younger POs studied at one of only a few colleges in the area, this behavior can be seen as an extension of existing friendship networks. Many of these POs knew each other before joining the DC and, presumably, socialized then. In addition, there is some evidence to suggest that some POs were attracted to the DC because friends were already working there.

The older POs do not constitute a clique per se by this criterion. As they are often opposed to the "professional" ideology, however, they may be seen as an antithetical force or ad hoc clique. Both groups of POs, the older veterans and the younger "professionals," have common interests that relate to the orderly functioning of the branch offices and this minimizes friction. Where conflicts arise between the two groups, in fact, the resolution has always centered on this common interest. In late 1974, for example, three young "professionals" who worked in one branch office had taken a photograph of themselves in a jail cell. The photograph was reproduced as a Christmas card and sent out to the parolees in their three caseloads. Two older POs who worked out of the same office objected to the Christmas card on the grounds that, first, sending Christmas cards to parolees constituted "fraternization" as prohibited by DC regulations, and second, that the portrayal of POs in a jail cell tended to demean all POs. These objections were formulated as an official grievance which, as a first step in the grievance procedure, was sent to the branch office supervisor. The supervisor brought all five POs together for an unofficial grievance meeting. At this meeting, the supervisor pointed out the consequences of an intraoffice feud. One of the younger "professionals" gave this account of the meeting:

> Terry laid it out this way. If we fight each other, we're going to bring heat down on the branch office. That means we're going to have to stop cheating on office hours, start observing the grooming and dress codes in the office—all that stuff, so we buried the hatchet. I admit that I go out of my way to piss those old dudes off and I get a kick out of it when they blow their cool. But I'm going to stop that stuff now because it's not worth it. We're all going to mind our own business, and if some beef comes up, we're going to take it to Terry.

The common interests of the two groups thus transcend and outweigh their differences. Confrontations have arisen in other branch offices and have been resolved similarly. After resolution, older and younger POs have been able to work together without friction.[20]

The major interests of the "professionals" center around an ideology which, as with social interaction patterns, appears to be an extension of their common educational experiences. The ideology stresses the importance of the client, the therapeutic ideal, and related concerns that are nominally associated with a professionalized role. For example:

> I'd like to see counseling emphasized. That includes more special programs and a better utilization of expertise. I've got counseling skills that the DC isn't utilizing.
>
> The DC doesn't realize that counseling or therapy requires a *milieu*. As a therapist, I have to isolate myself from many of the concerns of my job. I have to be two people, a therapist and a bureaucrat, and I have to keep those two roles separate.
>
> As far as I'm concerned, my professional obligations as a trained therapist and social worker are more important than my obligations as an employee of the DC.

And so forth and so on. The function of the "professionals" as a clique is to reinforce this ideology. POs who behave "professionally" are raised to a high status in the clique. When a PO's behavior is judged to be un-"professional," he is ostracized by the clique.

Aside from *propaganda,* however, the "professionals" appear to have little power as a coalition. During the firearms rebellion, for example, the clique played a minor role in communicating gossip among the offices. While this effort may have been some help, it is not clear that the rebellion would have failed without it. Where the daily routines of the branch offices are concerned, however, the "professionals" have neither the power to influence routines nor, or so it appears, the desire to wield this power.

There are two factors to explain this situation. First, ideological issues and tests seldom arise from the daily routines of the branch offices. In this sense, no office is more or less "professional" than any other. Second, the PO's interests as a member of the branch office team ordinarily outweigh his interests as a member of the clique. Branch office interests include the short-term concrete issues of when, under what conditions, and how much work the PO must do on a regular basis. The clique, in contrast, has interests only in long-term abstract issues. The power of the "professionals" accordingly is addressed to these issues and takes the form of ideological propaganda. When the PO encounters "trouble" then, he can count on his supervisor and officemates for concrete assistance because this is the nature of branch office power. In the same situation, the PO can expect only sympathy and moral support from the "professionals" because that is the nature of clique power. This factor is so important that, when a PO is denounced and ostracized by the "professionals," the outcaste status will have little effect on interactions with clique members or sympathizers in his own branch office during working hours.

As a final point, it should be noted that the "professional" ideology is manifested in an attitude towards certain types of paperwork. Margaret Gordon (1976) has noted that professional and paraprofessional POs in the Federal system are distinguished by their mean report-writing abilities and agilities. This is also a major difference between the older and younger POs. A typical statement from an older PO is:

> I don't understand what this "progress during the last period" shit is.
> The man didn't kill anybody and he didn't end up in prison. What
> do they expect of the guy? Do they want him to start attending
> church? I just write "satisfactory" or "unsatisfactory" in that space.
> That's the trouble with this job. There's getting to be too much
> bullshit.

In the context of the report his PO was referring to, "satisfactory" is a satisfactory response. Nevertheless, the form of the response can be expanded without altering its informational content. This is apparent in the typical statement of a "professional":

> My first report is always the hardest one to write. I have to cover all
> the factors, pathological, ecological, and developmental. The subse-

quent reports are easier because I have the first report to use as an outline. I take a lot of pride in my reports. I turned one in to Dr._____as a course project and he was very impressed with my thoroughness. He uses it as an example of a good report in his assessment classes. I'm proud of that. I spend a lot more time and effort when I know that another professional's going to be reading my reports. I suppose that's the same with your research, huh?[21]

The differential tolerance of paperwork in this case is attributed directly to the "professional" ideology: Some reports, especially those that are "clinical" in nature, must be taken seriously. Needless to say, even this attitude must be weighed against the interests of the branch office team, and where branch office interests conflict, the "professional" ideology gives way.

Power and Policy: The Conclusion

DC officials set policy. The branch office supervisors interpret policy and enforce their interpretations. POs execute the interpreted policy in a manner consistent with established routines and territories. Finally, the effects of the policy are evaluated by DC officials. This process has a special interpretation when viewed from the perspective of authority. One DC official described the actual decision-making mechanisms this way:

Before a staff meeting, we receive statements of problems. The first item on the agenda is a discussion of new problems. Someone proposes a solution to a problem and the [appropriate DC official] drafts a policy memorandum for the next meeting. The second item on the agenda is the approval of memoranda drafts from the previous meeting. Drafts are normally approved pro forma. The [appropriate DC official] then sends them out to the branch offices. The third item on the agenda is a report on the effects of policy memoranda. These are important. In an organization of this size and complexity, policies don't always have the desired effect. Some policies may have harmful side effects also. For example, a policy may result in so much extra work at the branch office level that it affects the performance of more important matters. The policy could detract from the performance of routine duties. When that happens, we may have to rethink the policy and perhaps even learn to live with the problem that the policy was designed to solve.

This is what happened to the no-firearms edict. The reaction to the policy at the branch office level created problems that outweighed the problems it was designed to solve. The general lesson of this episode is that the power of the branch office team is great enough to influence policy. The influence is direct and in the manner described by this DC official.

But on the other hand, we must not be deluded. Authority always entails a certain amount of power, so DC officials are not entirely powerless. *At any time and for any reason, the central authority of the bureaucracy could impose its will on the branch offices, even to the point of destroying them.* Assuming some rationality on the part of DC officials, it follows that it is not in the best interests of the central authority to destroy the branch offices. The reason for this is, obviously, that the branch offices serve a function. The rationale for bureaucratic federalism is that autonomous branches can respond to the immediate needs of local constituencies while still performing the greater, nonlocal function. The branch offices discharge the statutory obligations of the DC, that is, they perform the minimum functions required. In addition, the branch offices respond to the needs of local constituencies, especially the local branches of other criminal justice bureaucracies. As a result, interagency squabbles and political feuds are avoided, and in this sense, strong, autonomous branch offices serve the interests of DC officials. In fact, a number of DC officials have noted this:

> Compare us with California and you'll find that we're more efficient. It may take their parole authority over a year to revoke a parolee. That's because there's little cooperation among the criminal justice agencies. They're really not part of a system as we are. They're a monolithic bureaucracy. They can't respond efficiently. . . . Of course, that's why [California governor] tried to dismantle the parole authority. You won't find that happening in [this state].

Overall, the branch offices "deliver." They are responsive to the needs of the local constituencies and of the central authority. For the POs and supervisors, branch office autonomy is its own reward. To simplify matters, we can say that POs are interested in doing as little work as possible. Branch office autonomy serves this interest. So long as the branch office team "delivers," autonomy is maintained and POs are satisfied. Naturally, DC officials are also satisfied and this defines a status quo or bureaucratic dynamic. In the next few chapters, I will deal with the effect of status quo on parole outcomes.

NOTES

1. When I use the term "authority," I fall back on the Weberian definition which, for the bureaucratic context, is given by Gerth and Mills (1958: 197) as, "The principles of office hierarchy and of levels of graded authority mean a firmly ordered system of super- and subordination in which there is a supervision of the lower offices by the higher ones." This is Weber's Second Characteristic of a bureaucracy.

2. Similarly, Gerth and Mills (1958: 180) see Weber's definition of "power" as, "the chance of a man or of a number of men to realize their own will in a communal action even against the resistance of others who are participating in the action." While this definition is taken out of the bureaucratic context, its essence is general.

3. Much of the material attributed to officials comes from interviews with technicians. These DC officials were always more willing to discuss events and observations with me. On the whole, they have less of a personal stake in the outcome of power struggles, and hence, seldom have strong biases or opinions. The opposite is true of those DC officials who are directly responsible for the field operations.

4. By November 26th, all three daily newspapers had carried articles about the policy change. All three accounts quoted a single DC spokesman and all noted that, though unannounced, the policy had been implemented six weeks earlier. The delayed announcement suggests that the DC did not regard the policy change as "consequential" or important. In fact, it assumed importance only as a result of unrest in the branch offices. As an aside, it should be noted that each new DC administration in recent years has tried to disarm the POs and each has failed. According to one PO, "Everytime a new Director takes over, he tries to disarm us. That's why we've had so many Directors in the last few years." Finally, so there can be no mistake about the symbolism, POs were stripped of their badges by the same edict. Street-level bureaucrats use badges as tools, for obvious purposes, so the loss of a badge amounts to a direct loss of power.

5. Certain DC officials visit each branch office two or three times per month under normal circumstances. During the firearms rebellion, however, no DC official visited the two branch offices I was observing.

6. Although I see no need to do so, one might argue that the supervisors hold charismatic authority: The notion of "delivery," or performance, as covered later, is pertinent here.

7. One might legitimately ask, "Who is neutralizing whom?" Nevertheless, every branch office supervisor has this background. Matt recently retired, and in what cannot be regarded as a coincidence, he was replaced by another PO who had spent a number of years in the prosecutor's office before joining the DC.

8. And in addition, gives the supervisor some power. For example, I have seen a police department memorandum, marked "confidential," which instructs police officers not to arrest POs who are carrying firearms. The memorandum was issued at the height of the rebellion. It was distributed to all police precincts and to *all branch office supervisors.* This gives an accurate description of the power of the supervisors, two of whom came to the DC from the police department.

9. The civil service job descriptions for POs and supervisors.

10. I attended this meeting. One PO suggested that the supervisor did not want to discuss his motives because of my presence. I suspect that this is not true, however. The supervisor later discussed his motives with me and was, I believe, quite candid. Nevertheless, I decided not to attend any more branch office meetings. I relied on POs for reports of the agendas.

11. The site investigation report resembles in substance a presentence investigation report used in probation. This PO had obtained a copy of the model presentence investigation report used by U.S. probation officers. He was using the model as an outline for his site investigations.

12. The exception to this rule is the parolee who "shops around" for a PO. This is discouraged by the POs.

13. I suspect that this taboo had a great deal to do with the success of this study. As an outsider, not party to the norms of the branch offices, POs could openly discuss their office-mates with me. POs often asked me what their peers had said about them or about an episode. I never violated a confidence in this respect and many POs noted this factor in prologue; for example, "I could get in a lot of trouble if you repeated that. You've never repeated anything [that another PO has told you] to me, though, so I trust you."

14. Nearly all POs have substantial sidelines. Some are full time students, some have businesses, and some have other careers. In all cases, POs cite as one of the most desirable aspects of their job the flexible schedule and "free" time which allows them to have a substantial sideline. The sideline dominates the PO's official duties. Compare this with Weber's Fifth Characteristic of a bureaucracy, which, according to Gerth and Mills (1958: 198) is, "official activity demands the full working capacity of the official, irrespective of the fact that his obligatory time in the bureau may be firmly delimited."

15. I agree with this PO in principle, though not with his arithmetic. A PO can easily "paper" his caseload by a dozen parolees or so over a period of ninety days. In a later chapter, I will show how POs get rid of parolees but with another motive. Overall, the PO has great control of his caseload size.

16. This too is a tradition in the DC. Daniel Glaser (personal correspondence) relates an incident in which a PO was transferred to various cities around the state for this purpose.

17. Blau (1963) deals with this "exchange theory" in the bureaucratic context. Homans (1961) is generally agreed to be the source. I see no need to apply this

theory here, but rather, explain "collegial consultation" in terms of common interest. POs and supervisors have a direct and common interest in seeing that the branch offices function efficiently.

18. Wherever I set off this term in quotation marks, I am referring to the clique. "Professional" interests, for example, refers to the interests of the clique described here.

19. I am not making a value judgment here but merely describing the two groups of POs.

20. Another factor: The older POs are being replaced as they retire with POs who are better educated, and hence, sympathetic to the "professional" ideal.

21. Both POs are referring to the same report. As a rule of thumb, POs try to write as little as possible in reports that are used by the DC. However, POs often write reports for outside agencies. These include "extensive service" case reports for social service agencies and "progress reports" addressed to parole bureaucracies in other states. These reports give the PO a chance to demonstrate his "professional" skills at no cost. The topic of paperwork will be covered in detail in a later chapter.

Chapter 3

DISCRETION[1]

In the last chapter, I argued that power was enjoyed by groups or classes, not by individuals. This insight contradicts the conventional wisdom of criminology (e.g., Glaser, 1964), which tries to explain parole outcome at least in part as a function of PO discretion. Furthermore, parolees themselves believe that their POs are nearly omnipotent:

> Your PO can do whatever he wants and there's nothing you can do about it. If he says you're going back to the joint, that's all there is to it. All he's got to do is say that you didn't report or something like that. Who's going to say different? It's your word against his and nobody's going to believe you.

And finally, this insight contradicted my own initial impressions. From the beginning of this study, I had observed individual POs exercising gross discretionary power in case decisions.

As it turns out, individual POs do have substantial discretionary power but only in theory. In practice, the exercise of power is constrained by a set of structures. A PO may get away with exercising his power in a few cases, and in these cases, the effect is so striking as to give the impression that the PO is omnipotent. But in most cases, the PO is forced to restrain himself. The structural constraints relate to the bureaucratic status quo, particularly the power of the branch office team. When a PO exercises his discretion, he "brings heat down" on the branch office. All POs suffer. The branch office team restrains its members for the common good.

The clearest illustration of discretionary power is seen in the plea bargaining process. When a parolee is arrested, he faces two charges: one for the crime itself and one for the implicit violation of the parole contract. However, these charges are seldom separable or distinct, so the PO plays a crucial role in the plea bargaining session. According to a prosecuting attorney: "Even if I reduce the charge to a misdemeanor, the defendant can still be sent back to prison as a parole violator. He's got nothing to gain from the bargain. He won't plead guilty unless the PO guarantees that the parole violation warrant will be dropped. The PO has to go along with the deal."

No plea bargain can be made without the active participation and consent of the PO. POs are always included in the plea bargaining process, and not as a courtesy.[2] The discretionary power here is the power to "save" a client by holding out for a bargain that will not affect the client's status as a parolee. In one case, a parolee was given a probationary sentence in exchange for a guilty plea to a felony. Probation commenced only after the termination of parole, so the conviction had no effect on the parolee's status. More commonly, POs are able to force the prosecutor to reduce felony charges to misdemeanors. A parolee who pleads guilty to a misdemeanor need not be returned to prison.

In a related area, parole revocation, the PO exercises similar power. If a parolee is charged with a violation of the parole contract, he is given a quasi-judicial hearing on the charge. The PO must testify at this hearing, and of course, the outcome of the hearing depends largely on how the PO testifies. A DC official who serves as a judge in revocation hearings explained:

We can *force* a PO to issue a revocation warrant [against his wishes] but then the warrant has to go to hearing. The PO can sabotage the hearing just by hedging on his testimony. Unless the PO testifies positively and firmly, I have to dismiss the warrant. So of course, it wouldn't do us much good to force the PO to issue a warrant against one of his parolees. That's really a decision that has to be left up to the PO.

I witnessed more than one case where POs were forced to issue warrants but where the PO subsequently sabotaged the hearing. In many other cases, POs were *asked* to issue warrants of their own accord but refused.

Considering just these two areas, it is clear that POs enjoy substantial discretionary power. What is not immediately clear is that, if individual POs routinely exercised their powers, the bureaucratic dynamic described in the last chapter would collapse. The branch offices (and the people who work in them: POs and supervisors) and the central authority (DC officials) co-exist in a status quo that serves the interests of both. To maintain the status quo, the branch office teams enforce a set of unwritten rules which amount to structural constraints on discretion.

A related issue concerns the quality of a PO's interactions with his clients. Eisenstadt (1959; Eisenstadt and Katz, 1960) has coined the term "debureaucratization" to refer to the process whereby clients co-opt bureaucratic workers. If a PO is co-opted by a client, the status quo is threatened. Many DC officials see the co-optation of POs by parolees as a major problem. To some extent, the structural constraints on discretion are designed to minimize this problem.

In fact, most POs see themselves as counselors or therapists whose primary loyalty is to the client. One PO told me:

I don't *owe* my clients anything but there is a matter of professional ethics that I have to consider. If one of my clients tells me something in confidence, I don't always pass it along to the DC. I am a professional. I spent six years in school and another three years out there on the streets learning to do what I do. No DC honcho in (the state capitol) can tell me what's best for my client. That's what being a professional means.[3]

This comment is not atypical, although many POs temper their statements to include those rare cases where the client is "obviously dangerous."

DC officials tolerate and even encourage this attitude but insist at the same time that client loyalty be subordinated to organizational loyalty. There is always a potential conflict between these two loyalties, as illustrated by the following case. Richard, a former street gang member, had been working at a "good" job for over eight months. According to his PO, John, Richard was making an excellent adjustment to parole. One morning, John received a phone call from Richard's sister. She told John that Richard was carrying a pistol and that he might be planning an armed robbery. John and I visited Richard at his job that afternoon. Richard admitted carrying a pistol but denied that he was planning an armed robbery. He explained that his street gang was pressuring him to rejoin and that one gang member, Seaweed, had threatened his life. Although carrying a pistol is a serious violation of parole, John did not ask Richard to surrender the pistol. In fact, no report of the phone call from Richard's sister or the meeting with Richard was ever made. John explained his decision this way:

> Seaweed's a bad dude. He's the gang enforcer. What I *should* do is put out a warrant for Richard. That would be best for me and best for the DC. It wouldn't be best for Richard, though. I'm going to take a chance with him. I don't always do that. It depends on the dude and on the situation. If Richard gets caught with that piece, it's going to be frontpage stuff and that'll be bad for the DC. It'll be bad for me too because he might cop out and say I gave him permission. What I'm counting on is that if Richard gets caught, he'll leave my name out of it. He's been cool with me before.

This episode illustrates another aspect of discretion. In addition, it brings out three general points. First, organizational loyalty is usually related to publicity. As far as DC officials are concerned, a "good" PO is one who, among other things, does not embarrass the DC. Second, client loyalty often forces the PO to do things that at least run the risk of generating adverse publicity. Third, the PO often jeopardizes his career through client loyalty.

Few POs would have taken the risk that John took, yet most POs think of John as a "good" PO, a real "professional." DC officials, on the other hand, might say that POs like John are neither *fair* nor *competent*. These are euphemisms that DC officials use to describe organizational loyalty. While POs themselves do not admire *un*fairness or *in*competence in a literal sense, it turns out that they admire their peers who have been labeled unfair or incompetent. This is because by being fair and by being competent, a PO alters his relationship to his clients. He becomes an ideal DC employee rather than an ideal, "professional" PO.

As the data will show, a PO's potential discretion, or personal power, varies as a function of these labels. As fairness and competence are *only* labels, however, they can be manipulated by POs in a way that increases discretionary potential. This chapter is largely concerned with the ways POs manipulate their labels, and in turn, with *the ways these labels manipulate POs.* POs behave in ways that maximize their personal power in a few special cases, but to do this, POs surrender personal power that might be used in all cases.

Fairness

POs are labeled fair or unfair strictly on the basis of their behavior in a given situation. A DC official described fairness this way: "Don't forget the POs have two responsibilities, one to the ex-offender and one to the public. A fair PO stands behind his men 100 percent when they're innocent. When they're guilty, he turns his back on them. He balances his responsibility to the public."

POs themselves interpret fairness more cynically. They have another name for it. One PO told me:

Realistic is a better word for it. First off, I don't make distinctions between guilty and innocent men. I'll help a guilty man beat a rap if

I can and if he deserves a break, and I'll watch an innocent man go down the tubes if I have to. It's not that I don't want to help, it's that I can't. I can make a certain amount of trouble for the prosecutor but that's an unrealistic option. I'm only stalling off the inevitable. The prosecutor is going to get my man anyway and I'm only making a powerful enemy by stalling. What I do in a case like that is cooperate. Maybe I even give the prosecutor some moral support. Then I come out of it with a reputation for being fair. But that's not being fair, that's just being realistic.

Being fair or being realistic means knowing when the situation is hopeless. Some examples of hopeless situations are: "Anything with a gun or where somebody gets hurt. Heroin's okay but selling heroin's the same as murder. The prosecutor won't give my man a break in a case like that. He can't. The newspapers would crucify him."

A fair PO is loyal to his clients only until the situation becomes hopeless. An unfair PO in the same situation continues to resist the inevitable and thereby risks adverse publicity for the DC. The net effect of unfairness is to focus public attention

Table 3.1: Only a few situations are absolutely hopeless. Most are hopeless or promising in degree

Situation	Examples	Degree of Constraint on the PO
Absolutely hopeless	Murder Rape Weapons Assault Narcotics Sales	The PO has no freedom whatsoever. His behavior is totally constrained by the situation. If he "bucks the system," he will be denounced by his peers.
Marginally hopeless	Burglary Simple robbery	The PO has relatively little freedom.
Marginally promising	Narcotics possession	The PO has a relatively great degree of freedom.
Absolutely promising	All misdemeanors "Victimless" felonies	Freedom is greatest. The parolee will not ordinarily be returned to prison in these situations unless his PO is forced to "sacrifice" him for some reason.

on the failures of prisons, parole boards, and parole supervision agencies. The entire DC suffers, but as POs see it, most important of all: "You bring down heat on your partners and supervisor. You bring DC auditors into your [branch] office, and worse than that, reporters." Given this contingency, POs have a strong motivation for fair or realistic behavior. Unfairness damages the branch office.

A few situations are absolutely hopeless (see Table 3.1) but most are only hopeless in degree. In marginally hopeless situations, the PO can continue to fight for his client, and in so doing, can win the respect of his "professional" peers. For example, a PO told me: "Look here, if you were on an operating table, would you want a realistic surgeon? No! An unrealistic surgeon keeps on working until your heart stops and he doesn't worry about getting blood on the walls. Of course, that's just talk. You can carry anything to extremes." This was not an unusual comment. Most POs admire their peers who continue to fight for clients caught in hopeless situations. However, even the most rabid "professional" realizes that client loyalty can be carried too far.

The case of Lucas illustrates the principles underlying fairness. One of Lucas' clients was arrested on a highly publicized weapons charge. This situation was absolutely hopeless but Lucas felt that extenuating circumstances in the case demanded a reduced charge.[4] When the prosecutor refused to negotiate the charge, Lucas deliberately stalled the disposition of the case. The client was eventually returned to prison but not before Lucas' futile efforts were noted by the press. At the beginning of the incident, a PO told me: "I wish Lucas would quit diddling around with the dude. If he was my client, he'd be back in [prison] already. Any dude gets caught in [this] county with a piece gets revoked. That's all there is to it. Lucas is just getting himself and a lot of other people in trouble. He's not going to save the dude." Soon, POs began to feel that Lucas' behavior was exposing them, not the DC, to public ridicule. A few days later, when an exaggerated, sensationalized account of the case appeared in the newspapers, a PO said: "I've never been so pissed off in my life! Luke's done some crazy things before but never like this. He's putting every one of us out there on front street. If he thinks he's going to get away with this, he's wrong. I'm not going to complain, but I know a half-dozen other POs who are."

As a result of lobbying by other POs, Lucas was relieved of his caseload and transferred to another parole district. Because POs think of such transfers as demotions, it can be said that Lucas' behavior was denounced by his peers and punished by his superiors. The transfer had the collateral effect of removing Lucas from his branch office, a factor noted by his supervisor: "I couldn't have him working here any more because of the morale problem. We're a team in this office. Everybody does his share of the work. Everybody does what's expected of them. My POs depend on each other for that. Luke just isn't a very dependable person. He proved that."

Lucas spent six weeks working his new district and then resigned. Two years after this episode, POs still spoke badly of Lucas and often cited his behavior as the model of unfairness.

This episode demonstrates, first, that situations are realistic or unrealistic, hopeful or hopeless, only in terms of potential for adverse publicity. POs who refuse to abandon clients in hopeless situations soon acquire reputations for unfairness. Second, while POs generally admire peers who "buck the system," POs will denounce any peer who carries idealism to the extreme. This is because extremism endangers the image of all POs, and more importantly, brings "heat" down on the branch office. Thus, while individual POs enjoy potentially gross personal power, its exercise is restricted to only a few situations.

Competence

Fairness is a relatively clear and concrete term. Competence is not. A DC official, for example, told me:

A competent PO knows when his clients are lying. He doesn't run around half-cocked, tilting at windmills. He's sure of his facts before he jumps on somebody. Frankly, one of the biggest problems we have is that some POs get too close to their clients. A PO like that isn't competent. You can't make good judgments when you're emotionally involved.

Other DC officials defined *in*competence similarly: A lapse in judgment resulting from an emotional involvement with a client. POs seem to be familiar with this notion but many dispute a key point. One PO said:

> You never know when a client's lying. Maybe you can test him out by asking him something you can check up on. If it turns out he lied, you know he's lying about other things too. But what if he passes your test? That doesn't mean he's not going to lie about other things. You never know when a client's lying but you never admit that. If somebody asks you about a client, you make something up and hope you get away with it. Anytime a PO says something definite about a client, the PO has to tell a lie.

POs routinely confessed to "lying." Social psychologists might describe this behavior more sympathetically as reinterpretation or reconstruction of reality: Argumentation. For example, a PO might embellish the facts of a case when discussing it with the prosecutor:

> Washington's not a criminal. He's sick. He needs treatment. The charge against him is substantially petty anyway. Would you call that a burglary? I'm going to try to get him probation on this. Then I'll get him into a drug rehabilitation program. . . .
>
> Brown didn't go along of his own accord. They forced him into it. I talked to Brown and I think I can get him to cooperate with you. If he testifies against the others, can you give him a break?

In effect then, when a PO tries to intercede with the prosecutor on behalf of a client, the PO is "lying."

The point of this argument is that the PO's ability to get away with "lying" depends largely on his reputation for competence. The better his reputation, the more credible are his "lies." In one case illustrating this point, a PO was contacted by a police

detective for routine information on a parolee. Tony, the PO,
first phoned the parolee's home. He then sent a memorandum
to the detective saying that he had *seen* the parolee that day
and that the parolee was making excellent progress. It turned
out later that the parolee had absconded and was in jail in
another state. Tony therefore could not have seen the parolee as
he said he had. Tony's supervisor described this incident:

> What happened was that Tony called up the client's brother and the
> brother lied to Tony. He said that the client was at work but that
> everything was fine. That's what Tony should have put in his
> report—that he talked to the *brother*. Instead, Tony was dumb
> enough to stake his career on the brother's word. Now what hap-
> pened after that was that this detective tells everybody in the police
> department about Tony. Tony looks incompetent, I look incompe-
> tent, everybody in the DC up to and including the Director looks
> incompetent. We have to work with the police and that's hard when
> they think we're an incompetent outfit. Tony knows he's got a bad
> reputation. He should have known better. He never should have
> taken the word of the parolee's brother about something so impor-
> tant.

The POs who commented on this incident were familiar with
the consequences of Tony's behavior but most emphasized
another point. One PO said:

> They don't really think Tony lied even though that's what really
> happened. He never called that guy's brother but they prefer to
> think he did. They want to think it's a case of a PO being chumped
> by one of his guys. They don't want to think that Tony's dishonest.
> They want to think he's a chump. See, the police think that POs are
> a bunch of do-gooders. Tony's problem is that he's been tagged with
> that before, so they're always checking up on him. Hell, I vouch for
> some of my guys too but I don't have to worry about people laying
> for me like they lay for Tony. Tony's the type of PO who gets close
> to his guys. People see him doing that and right away they think he's
> a do-gooder. Hell, I think Tony's one of the best POs I've ever
> known.

This was a typical opinion. Many POs actually suspected entrapment, suspected that the policeman had known the parolee's whereabouts all along but called Tony only on the chance that Tony might lie.

Another version of what "really happened" comes from Tony himself. He refused to discuss the case per se but offered this assessment of its consequences: "I still sit in on plea bargaining sessions but they don't listen to me anymore. It's frustrating. The Public Defender's not looking out for my client's interests, and when I try to, the Public Defender and the prosecutor tell me to butt out." Tony resigned from the DC shortly after making this statement. He felt that he could no longer represent his clients effectively. In fact, formal or informal plea bargaining sessions present the PO with his greatest opportunity to "lie" for his clients. When this forum is denied him, the PO is essentially powerless.

Congruencies in this and similar episodes support a few generalizations on the subject of competence. For example, it is apparent that competence is not a concrete entity. It is a mystique. Furthermore, while DC officials equate incompetence with gullibility, POs have a more complicated, more cynical interpretation. From their perspective, POs who have been labeled do-gooders are closely scrutinized. This scrutiny inevitably leads to the discovery of "lies," and to the stigma of incompetence.

Regarding scrutiny, it should be noted that the stigma of incompetence has a similar effect inside the branch office. Police and prosecutors keep a sharp eye on POs who are suspected incompetents and this places an extra burden on the branch office supervisor. In Tony's case, for example, the supervisor was instructed via memorandum from a high DC official to scrutinize Tony's future behavior. In the extreme, then, an incompetent PO is subject to scrutiny even from his officemates. For example, supervisors have remarked:

> My biggest problem is taking the flack for an incompetent PO. When
> I have an incompetent man working in this office, I have to watch

him night and day. If he pulls some bone headed stunt, I have to catch it before it gets out of this office. If somebody outside catches it, it looks like I'm not doing my job.

He's a shit magnet. Don't get me wrong, I like the kid but he's more trouble than he's worth. Actually, I guess he's a pretty good PO. He grates a lot of people in the police department the wrong way though and he's got a reputation for fouling up. When a PO gets a reputation like that, it makes more work for the supervisor.

But the incompetent PO may interpret his supervisor's scrutiny as harrassment. This perception will be aggravated by the changed attitudes and behaviors of his office-peers. In the long run, the stigmatized PO will come to feel that he is no longer part of the branch office team.

The effects of stigmatization are best seen in the practice of *covering*. POs are often required to observe court hearings involving their clients. As the PO takes no formal part in the proceedings, however, he can easily write a report without actually attending the hearing. If two POs have to be in court on the same day then, one PO can attend both hearings and thereby *cover* his partner. If a PO has been stigmatized, however, the situation changes:

I can't cover the courts for Mike anymore. Auslander's checking up on Mike all the time, and if I cover him, we'll both get in trouble. All Auslander's got to do is pop his head in the courtroom and see that Mike's not there. Then Mike's in trouble. . . . Anyway, how can Mike pay me back? I don't want him covering my cases. Auslander's on his ass, Judge Kraft's on his ass. . . . If I let him cover my cases, he'd get us both in trouble. Mike's going to have to cover himself from now on.

Mutual covering saves each PO on the branch office team a number of day's work in every month. The goal of the branch office team, of course, is to minimize the time and effort that members must devote to inconsequential but official duties and obligations. Arrangements of this sort are quite common. But, of course, stigmatized POs must be excluded from such arrangements, and in effect then, must be excluded from sharing in the benefits of the team:

The Mystique of Rep

Fairness and competence are reputations or labels, or as POs themselves say, "reps." Novice POs are ordinarily considered to be fair until their behavior in a hopeless situation proves them otherwise. POs do not actually have to build reps for fairness. Instead, a positive rep for fairness comes with the job. The novice PO maintains this rep simply by being realistic.

Competence is another matter. Novice POs are ordinarily assumed to be *in*competent. Novices build increasingly stronger reps for competence as time passes and as they begin more and more to successfully interact with peers, DC officials, police, and prosecutors. Under optimal conditions, a novice PO will need a year or more to convince all of these people that he is competent.

To build a strong rep, the novice PO must be *informative, hyperfair,* and *selective.* These component terms will ordinarily describe the quality of the PO's interactions and relationships with outside agencies. When these terms are examined closely, however, it is apparent that they also describe the quality of the PO's relationships with clients. In effect, the PO's relationships with clients becomes an important structural constraint on discretion.

To begin with, an *informative* PO is simply one who feeds information into the criminal justice system. Some of this information will be useful, for example, the "tip." Many POs encourage their clients to become informants for this purpose. One credentials conscious PO summed up this situation: "The best degree to have so far as status is concerned is an M.S.W. But I'd rather have three dependable snitches than three college degrees. When you come up with a hot tip, the boys downtown think you're on the ball." A tip not only strengthens the PO's rep but also indebts the tip recipient to the PO. A PO who has amassed a number of favors with the police and prosecutors will ordinarily have enormous discretionary power.[5]

While information of this type is useful to the criminal justice system, POs more often feed useless information into the system. These data typically consist of trivial information the PO has collected from his clients. For example, I overheard one PO tell a client:

> Look here, Ray. Why don't you give me your chick's address. I won't hassle her or anything, but if they ever pick you up down there, I can say, "Yeah, so what? I know where Ray is. He's down there visiting his chick and her address is such-and-such." Then I won't look like a chump. You know, it'll look like you asked my permission first.

While useless to the system, this information contributes to the overall air of competence the PO tries to exude. I have never met a PO who did not collect trivial data, and in fact, most POs keep notebooks or index card files near their telephones. The PO in this example was candid about the value of this information:

> Some POs will tell you they use this stuff to track down absconders but that's foolish. Absconders don't leave forwarding addresses. Collecting this stuff is like keeping two sets of books—one for me and one for the I.R.S. I use this stuff to bluff somebody once in a while but mostly I use it to make my reports look intelligent.

Bluffing is always done with caution. If the PO's rep is strong enough, his bluffs are seldom called. An incompetent PO, on the other hand, cannot ordinarily bluff even his own supervisor.

In addition to being informative, the competent PO must be *hyperfair*. A fair PO abandons his clients when the situation becomes hopeless but a hyperfair PO actually turns on his clients in hopeless situations. One PO told me:

> You know why Auslander likes me? Because every so often I help him burn one of my men. It's usually a case where I can't help the

man anyway but Auslander doesn't know that. Then the next time I ask him to give one of my men a break, he thinks he owes me a favor. He's got the idea that when I think one of my men is guilty, I'm going to help him pull the switch. A rep like that doesn't hurt.

Like delivering a hot tip, being hyperfair may indebt the police and prosecutor to the PO.

A hyperfair PO cooperates with the prosecutor by lending moral support, by leaking clinical data that the prosecutor could not legally obtain, and in rare cases, by prejudicing the defense attorney. In one case reported by an informant but independently verified, a PO gave both the prosecutor and the defense attorney copies of a clinical report that diagnosed a client as a "violent psychopath." As a result, the defense attorney was prejudiced against the client and could not vigorously represent the client during plea bargaining. More commonly, however, the PO behaves hyperfairly by using his influence with the client to coerce a guilty plea:

> The way plea bargaining works, the prosecutor and the Public Defender sit down and decide on a reasonable charge and sentence. Well, the parolee wasn't party to the negotiations, so he usually balks at first. That's where I come in. I go down and advise the parolee to take the deal. I've got clout with the parolee because I can tell him I'll drop the DC warrant if he deals. That way, he's got a clean sheet when he goes up for parole the next time. It also means sometimes that the parolee can get out of jail on bond, which he can't do if he's got a DC warrant pending. That's a big thing sometimes. Now what do I get out of the deal? The prosecutor gets a good impression of me and maybe I can ask him for a favor in the future.

The PO, in fact, is central to the plea bargaining process. Hyperfairness is absolutely essential to the orderly functioning of the criminal courts. In return, the PO builds a strong rep and accumulates favors.

Finally, in addition to being informative and being hyperfair, the competent PO must be *selective*. Like being hyperfair, being selective entails helping the prosecutor at the expense of the client. Unlike being hyperfair, however, being selective is not confined only to hopeless situations. Instead, the selective PO routinely underrepresents some clients and overrepresents others regardless of the leeway in the situation. In one case, for example, a PO testified as a character witness for a client. The PO later told me:

> I don't do that often. If I testify for a client, the judges know that the client is all right. I've got a good rep with the judges because I'm selective. But if I testified for every one of my clients who got into a little scrape, the judges wouldn't trust me anymore. They'd think I'd turned into a goddam social worker. You can't save everybody. If you try, you end up not being able to save anybody.[6]

The epithets "social worker" and "do-gooder" are used to describe incompetent POs. To avoid these labels, and consequently, the stigma of incompetence, POs are forced to sacrifice some clients caught in marginal or even absolutely realistic situations (See Table 3.1).

The major implication of selectivity is that the PO must decide which clients to save and which clients to sacrifice. This decision is determined to a great extent by personal considerations, which are not central to this argument, and by organizational contexts, which will be discussed in the next chapter. What is certain is that POs secure and maintain strong reps by being selective. This in fact is the major criterion of competence used by DC administrators:

> Competence boils down to interpersonal skills. A PO has to be able to size up his clients. In those cases where POs went out on limbs for clients—and had the limbs cut from under them—a lack of interpersonal skills is at fault. I distrust POs who use superlatives in every case, who go out on limbs for every client. That suggests to me that the PO can't distinguish between good and bad clients.

POs who exercise discretion selectively are seen as more competent than POs who exercise discretion in every case.

The PO's motive for being selective is to increase his discretionary power. Once his rep for competence is established, the PO enjoys gross discretionary power. To maintain this rep, however, the PO must exercise his discretion only selectively. Thus, the PO's enjoyment of personal power is constrained by the rep building process.

POs learn selectivity through trial and error or through imitating successful peers. In some cases, the supervisor, as the elder statesman and spiritual father of the branch office, will take the novice PO aside and explain the facts of life. I observed one such *tête-à-tête* first-hand:

> Look, Larry, I want to talk to you about this request for an early discharge. Now I'm sure that Jackson deserves an early discharge. You've documented that in your report and I don't question it. But the fact is that you're writing too many of these things. They're going to start questioning your abilities sooner or later. You're going to get a reputation for being soft and that's going to cause trouble for you.

Other POs have related substantively similar anecdotes. In each case, the novice PO is taken aside and advised by his supervisor to be selective.

Given that a PO must be selective, the obvious question is: How do POs decide that certain parolees are worthy of "saving"? There appears to be no single answer to this question. POs interact with parolees over a long period of time. At some point in the interaction, the PO decides that a certain parolee is *special.* A case that illustrates this phenomenon concerns a PO who perjured himself to *alibi* a client. After testifying in court, the PO told me:

> It wasn't something I did without thinking about it first. The dude is an apprentice—some sort of trade. He's two months away from finishing the program. I figured he needed a break. If I didn't testify, he would have gone back to the joint for five or six years. I'd have to start all over on him when he got out. He'd be too old for an apprenticeship by then. I'm glad I did it but it's not something I'd do for just anybody. You can only do that for a dude you really

trust. If this dude had copped out after I testified, I'd be finished here. I knew this dude would stick to his story no matter what happened. We've got a really close relationship.

It was fairly common knowledge in the branch office that the PO had perjured himself. The norm of noninterference kept POs from openly discussing the case, however. More importantly, the perjurer had an outstanding rep for competence, so no one doubted his ability to come out of the incident unharmed. As far as the perjurer himself was concerned, this exercise of purely personal discretionary power was his prerogative. This was his *special* client, and because he had established himself as a team player, the PO had earned the right to "save" his special client. The other members of the office team accepted this without question.

We can see that selectivity is the most important component of the rep building process. Selectivity increases the PO's discretionary power while at the same time limiting its use. Selectivity means that the PO only rarely tries to "save" clients. Recalling that the indiscriminate exercise of discretion threatens the status quo, we see that selectivity also reinforces the bureaucratic dynamic. A PO who is selective will not often disrupt the status quo, and in this sense, the quality of competence, as defined by DC officials, takes on a new meaning.

In the branch offices, we see a similar effect. A PO with a strong rep is ipso facto a team player, while, conversely, a PO with a weak rep is not. The team player only rarely tries to "save" clients. The other members of the team can excuse or pardon the infrequent disruptive act because the disrupter is otherwise a team player, and of course, because the other members have *special* clients too. An occasional disruptive act is the reward for being a team player. But if a PO has a weak rep, which is the same as saying that he is not a full-fledged member of the branch office team, disruption is not tolerated.

Summary: How the System Works in
General and a Conclusion

The preceding argument has dwelt on the PO's dealings with other criminal justice agencies, especially the police and prosecutor. POs also spend time working with social welfare agencies. The constraints on discretion are generally the same, however. The case of Reynaldo illustrates the basic principles in another context. When I first met Reynaldo, he was one of Bob's clients. Reynaldo wanted to earn a high school diploma, so he asked Bob to sponsor him for admission to a special education program. Bob refused without any explanation. A short time later, Reynaldo moved to another part of the city and was transferred to Whitney's caseload. Whitney immediately sponsored Reynaldo for admission to the special program. When I discussed this changeabout with Reynaldo, he expressed the opinion that Bob was prejudiced against Spanish-speaking parolees. Whitney disagreed with Reynaldo's assessment of Bob, however:

> No, Bob's straight. You don't realize that a PO has to be careful about who he sponsors for some of these programs. If you send a real jag down, the program might take it out on the rest of your caseload. I can't show you Reynaldo's records but he's got some things in his past that make him look like a bad risk for this program. I had to do some real talking to get him in. Now I've been around here a long time and I have some clout. I can afford to take a chance on Reynaldo. But Bob's a rookie. He has to be careful.

Narcotics offenders, check artists, and burglars are bad risks because of their relatively high recidivism rates. These parolees will often be denied access to the best programs for an obvious reason. I heard one PO tell a high risk parolee: "Hey man, that program is expensive. You could be back in [prison] two weeks from now and all the money they spent on you would be wasted. You show me a year of good behavior on the streets and then I'll think about sponsoring you."

Parolees can also be denied opportunities because their "profiles" are inappropriate. For example: "Hooker needs a job bad. I'd send him down for this one but his profile's wrong. They're looking for young married dudes."

Profiles are most important when the agency has an unofficial "target" clientele. POs present their best faces to the agencies by scrupulously observing the target guidelines. If necessary, the agency can enforce its guidelines either indirectly, as Whitney described, or directly by complaining to the DC about the PO. The complaint would naturally affect the PO's rep adversely.

The effects of these structural constraints on outcome are obvious. Two parolees may be arrested for the same crime, yet depending upon their POs, one might be returned to prison while the other continues on parole. The difference in outcomes can be attributed to individual characteristics of the two POs and to the differential effects of the structural constraints on discretion. The two parolees will differ only in that one is a *special* parolee. In the general situation, outcomes are attributed to the strength of the PO's rep. A PO with an established rep can demand a larger share of social service for his clients. Again, this larger share will be distributed unevenly within the PO's caseload. A PO in the process of building a strong rep, on the other hand, must settle for a meagre share of social services for his clients.

But the larger question here concerns the doctrine of collective goods and collective action. Each PO is a potentially powerful individual. The doctrine of collective action holds that individuals will *not* sacrifice *personal* good for the sake of the *collective* good. The reason for this is that the individual will share in the collective good regardless of whether he makes personal sacrifices or not.[7] The question then is: Why do POs sacrifice their gross personal power, the potential discretionary power enjoyed in every case decision? The obvious answer is that POs sacrifice personal power for collective power, but again, why?

There are many plausible explanations but only one deserves special consideration here. First, according to one supervisor:

> Sure, my POs gripe about these unwritten rules but that's only talk. We've got a pretty good deal here and they know it. We're running this office more or less as an autonomous operation. The DC leaves us pretty much alone but the reason why they leave us alone is that

we obey the unwritten rules. We're on the honor system. We're gentlemen.

So *collective good* may be defined as the power that accrues to the branch office team. All POs and the supervisor share in this good. Concretely, the power of the branch office team is the minimization of time and effort that must be devoted to trivial duties and obligations.

But to maintain the collective good, each member of the branch office team must obey a set of unwritten rules which have been described here as structural constraints. If even one member of the branch office team decides not to submit to these structural constraints, the collective good disappears. Thus, while the rule-breaking PO realizes the full potential of his personal power, he pays a price in terms of collective power. Even if the rule-breaker is willing to pay this price, his office-mates will not be willing to let him sacrifice the collective good. When an auditor comes into the branch office, even when the audit concerns only the rule-breaker, *all* POs suffer.

We may contrast this with the more common collective goods situation. The Old Testament God, for example, was generally unwilling to punish all men for the sins of a few.[8] Similarly, a teacher is generally unwilling to punish all students for the misbehavior of a few. The class recreation period is never cancelled because one or two students have misbehaved. Cancellation punishes the innocent along with the guilty.

On the other hand, DC officials make no distinctions. When a PO disrupts the status quo, the DC audits his case files and while the auditor is in the branch office, all POs suffer: "I couldn't keep our appointment yesterday because I had office hours scheduled. . . . They got some snooper down here going through Tony's records. I had to cut my classes this morning. I hope he's out of here by the end of the week."

So when even one PO disrupts the status quo, the collective good vanishes. POs can no longer cheat on office hours, cut corners on official duties, or share in any of the collective good that accrues to members of the branch office team. The exception to this general rule is the disruptive act of a PO with a strong rep. In this case, we see that it is the rep per se which excuses the act. DC officials are reluctant to provoke a confrontation with a full-fledged member of the team.

In the final analysis, the POs themselves enforce the unwritten rules and structural constraints on discretion. Their motive relates directly to the collective good. Their ability to enforce the rules relates to the power of the branch office team. As the supervisor is a member, and as the supervisor controls work standards, enforcement is a simple matter. Beyond this, by denouncing a PO who consistently disrupts the status quo, the branch office team announces to the central authority that the team will not resist an official censure of the disrupter. DC officials can then proceed without fearing a confrontation. We may contrast this situation with the case of the firearms rebellion. In that situation, DC officials hesitated because they feared the branch office teams.

The remaining questions concern the *special clients*. Given the status quo, we see that a PO uses his discretionary power to benefit only a few special clients. In a caseload of one hundred, it is unlikely that more than ten clients would be special. In the next chapter, I will examine the process whereby an ordinary parolee achieves this status.

NOTES

1. Substantial portions of this chapter appeared as "How structural variables constrain the parole officer's use of Discretionary power," *Social Problems*, 1975, *23*(2). They are reprinted by permission of *Social Problems* and the Society for the Study of Social Problems.

2. I have observed thirty-two plea bargaining sessions in three years. There is some ambiguity in definition, however. What I actually observed were meetings attended by PO, prosecutor, and defense attorney, where court proceedings were discussed and where some agreement was reached. Judges were never present at these meetings. I assume that there is a parallel meeting between judge, prosecutor, and defense attorney where the agreement reached earlier is formalized. POs rarely attend these formal meetings.

3. The PO was not referring to the clique here. Again, when I refer to the clique, the name is set off in quotation marks: the "professionals."

4. What distinguished this case from most others was that the parolee was *absolutely* innocent. His crime consisted of being in the wrong place at the wrong time. Lucas' mistake was considering this factor at all. Innocence and guilt occur independently of the relative hopelessness of the situation. POs are expected to behave in a manner appropriate to this criterion, that is, the PO is expected to be *realistic,* regardless of the client's innocence or guilt.

5. Tips ordinarily concern drug trafficking. Given the proliferation of narcotic control agencies, a PO can make his tips serve double or triple duty.

6. Returning to the parole agency-university analogy, it seems to me that many academics are selective when recommending undergraduates to graduate schools or when recommending new Ph.D.s for jobs. "You can't save everybody. If you try. . . ."

7. Doctrines of collective good are a recurrent theme in Western culture. Much of the Old Testament, for example, deals with the problem of sinners who nevertheless were allowed to share the collective good. Bountiful harvests were shared by all, regardless of their behavior. Olson (1965) develops the doctrine in an economic context and Coleman (1973) applies it to a more general context of social exchange.

8. For example, recall that Noah was the last good man on earth. His family, not-so-good, benefited only because God realized that Noah would be punished if his family were not also saved from the Flood. My impression of the Old Testament is that God destroyed entire social units only when every member of the unit had it coming.

Chapter 4

PAROLEE TYPES

The last two chapters have described a bureaucratic dynamic, or status quo. Briefly, we may say that POs and supervisors are interested in doing as little work as possible. DC officials, on the other hand, are interested in minimizing political squabbles with other criminal justice bureaucracies and in maintaining a positive public image for the DC. These two sets of interests coincide in the autonomy of the branch offices. By permitting the branch offices to operate autonomously, DC officials permit POs and supervisors to realize their interests. If the POs and supervisors do not behave in a way that protects the interests of DC officials, the DC officials can restrict the autonomy of the branch offices. To protect the interests of DC officials, and thereby to protect their own interests, POs and supervisors recognize a set of unwritten rules.

Nevertheless, we saw in the last chapter that individual POs enjoy a potentially great power and that they exercise this

power only to benefit a few *special* clients. This raises the issue
of parolee types. There is a type of parolee who, to the PO at
least, deserves special consideration in the outcome process.
More important, however, there is a type of parolee who causes
trouble for the bureaucratic dynamic, who threatens the status
quo. POs are expected to recognize and deal with these troublemakers.

The notion of *typing* human beings has lately acquired pejorative images and symbols. Yet client typing is the sine qua non
of rational, bureaucratic service delivery. As Merton (1940:
561) notes: "The generality of [bureaucratic] rules requires the
constant use of *categorization*, whereby individual problems and
cases are classified on the basis of designated criteria and are
treated accordingly." So without client typing, there would be no
service bureaucracy. The service bureaucracy classifies or types its
clients on the basis of client needs, and in so doing, the service
bureaucracy maximizes the impact of its scarce resources.

Unfortunately, service bureaucracies are not Weberian-ideal
machines. Sometimes the bureaucratic worker breaks rules, and
as this relates to client typing, we see that the bureaucratic
worker may type a client, not on the basis of client needs, but
on the basis of some personal need. When this happens, a typing
scheme no longer promotes the rational, efficient pursuit of
legitimate goals. Instead it addresses the needs and problems of
the bureaucratic workers.

Bureaucratic dysfunction in this sense comes about because,
to the worker, short-run operational problems are more important than long-run abstract goals. If short-run problems are not
solved efficiently, the worker is held personally accountable.
When the long-run goals of the bureaucracy are not met, on the
other hand, no personal blame accrues to the worker.

In the DC, we may say that the long-run goals of the
bureaucracy amount to rehabilitating those parolees who are
amenable to rehabilitation while simultaneously protecting society from those who are not. An ideal parolee typing scheme
then should be concerned only with two specific parolee types.
The first type is to be controlled while the second type is to be

rehabilitated. This scheme is justified because it promotes an efficient discharge of the DC's two legitimate goals.

The ideal is seldom realized, however, and there are two reasons for this. First, parolee typing occurs at the lowest level of the bureaucratic hierarchy. By virtue of their low position in the hierarchy, the POs who actually do the typing are affected by a long list of operational problems. These problems will be called generally, "trouble." In a more specific sense, POs have an interest in the operation of the branch office: Doing as little work as possible. Trouble is any ·condition that threatens this interest. Moreover, as the interests of DC officials are tied directly to the interests of POs, trouble is any condition that threatens the status quo.

The second reason why the typing scheme dysfunctions is that there is no simple means of evaluating a typing decision. I demonstrated in the last chapter that the PO's overall performance, in contrast, is easily evaluated. A "good" PO is both fair and competent. These qualities relate directly to trouble in that a "good" PO solves routine problems as they arise, and of course, the DC knows who its "good" POs are. But the actual typing decisions cannot be evaluated except indirectly. Presumably, a PO whose decisions are consistently "correct" will appear to be both fair and competent, and thus, will appear to be a "good" PO. So because the PO's typing decisions per se cannot be evaluated, and because his overall performance can be evaluated, and because it is evaluated on the basis of how efficiently he handles trouble, the PO is encouraged to use the typing scheme to handle trouble.

The importance of parolee typing to outcome is apparent. Certain outcomes become more or less likely as a result of the certain typing decisions. And as the typing decision occurs at the very beginning of the parole experience, outcomes are largely predetermined, with no allowance for retyping. As the typing scheme is used to solve routine problems, or trouble, outcome is seen as a function of these routine problems. Most important, outcome need not be a function of the trouble actually caused by or attributable to the parolee, but rather, may be a function of how much trouble the PO *expects* from the parolee.

Generally, the major routine problem faced by POs is controlling parolees. The deeper problem is that the DC expects a degree of control which often exceeds the PO's resources and legal authority. One PO explained this: "A lot of these things the DC asks you to do are illegal. There's no way you can force your parolees to do them. What you do is you *persuade* your parolees to do these things. You try to point out to the parolees how those things are in their best interests."

But if the PO can*not* control his parolees, "trouble" results. The PO has failed to solve a common, routine problem and this will be counted against him when the DC evaluates his performance. Fortunately, for the PO at least, the parolee typing process can be used as a mechanism of control. If the PO can diagnose or recognize a "trouble"-maker early in the parole experience, he can make a typing decision that will enhance his control over an otherwise uncontrollable parolee.

A second routine problem faced by POs relates to the so-called special treatment programs. The DC receives federal funding for the treatment of certain types of parolees. Continued funding depends upon the number of parolees in need of treatment. This translates into a routine problem when the the DC sets de facto quotas for certain parolee types. POs could solve this problem simply by referring clients to the programs at random. However, POs are able to kill two birds with one stone by using the appropriate typing decision to rid themselves of potentially "trouble"-some but nevertheless "treatable" parolees. In this case, one decision solves two problems.

Finally, a more complicated and abstract problem relates to the nature of "professionalism." Most POs are counselors or therapists by virtue of training and disposition. Most took jobs with the DC in fact because they wanted to do counseling work and "parole counseling" was the only opportunity.[1] On the job, however, the would-be therapist discovers that his duties center around a set of bookkeeping chores. Alienation is minimized by extracurricular counseling that, for all practical purposes, the

PO does on his own time. This problem requires a certain parolee type and an associated typing decision. This last parolee type, of course, is the PO's special client. In the last chapter, I demonstrated that, by an unwritten rule, a PO could exercise his discretion on behalf of a client only infrequently, that is, he is allowed to have only a few special clients. The process by which a parolee becomes a special client is of some theoretical interest.

The Typing Process

The parolee-typing process has four discrete stages. *First*, the PO receives a skeleton dossier on a prospective parolee. The PO reviews the skeleton dossier and may type the parolee on the basis of these data alone. *Second,* the PO conducts a site investigation of the new parolee's home environment. The PO may type the parolee on the basis of data collected during the site investigation. *Third,* after reviewing the skeleton dossier and conducting a site investigation, the PO meets his new client for the first time. If the PO has not already typed the parolee, the initial interview might be used to confirm or disconfirm theories about the parolee. For certain typing decisions, the process ends at this stage. For other decisions, a *fourth* stage is required. This usually amounts to a period of time during which the PO and parolee interact in appropriate roles. However, in each of the four stages of the typing process, decisions are made on the basis of how much "trouble" the PO expects from the new parolee.

THE SKELETON DOSSIER

Prisoners are released on parole from two to six months after receiving a favorable verdict from the parole board. During this waiting period, the PO receives a skeleton dossier which contains (1) a police history or "rap" sheet, (2) a recent photograph of the parolee, and (3) a personal assessment of the parolee written by a prison social worker.[2] The personal assessment is also called a "parole plan" because a major portion of it concerns the parolee's future plans.

POs ignore most of the data found in the skeleton dossier. Regarding one new client's parole plan, for example, a PO told me: "That's garbage. Most of us [POs] have written those assessments ourselves and we know that certain things are obligatory. You have to say certain things just to fill up the white space on the form." This statement is the conventional wisdom among POs.

An exception to this rule is the rap sheet. POs agree that the rap sheet contains a great deal of valuable information: "The rap sheet tells you how much trouble you can expect from the client. You can tell what types of crime he's into and whether he's committed to a criminal career. You can also tell if he runs with a gang. The reason why the rap sheet is so important is that past behavior is the best predictor of future behavior."

The PO can also determine from the rap sheet whether the new client was ever on parole before. If so, the PO can often determine whether the new client was a troublemaker in his former parole experience.

THE SITE INVESTIGATION

The site investigation usually amounts to checking out the names and addresses listed in the parole plan. The PO then files a site investigation report stating briefly that the parole plan appears to be essentially truthful. It is interesting to note the value that different actors see in the site investigation report. First, one of the highest officials in the DC told me:

> The site investigation report is used strictly as a bookkeeping device. It signals our computer to transfer the case from [a prison] to a parole supervision caseload. The site investigation itself is quite important, however, A few years ago, a prisoner was paroled to a nonexistent address. That happens only rarely, but when it does happen, it's extremely embarrassing. We emphasize the site investigation itself primarily to guard against that sort of thing.

To DC officials then, the site investigations are important only in that they eliminate low-probability, high-cost mistakes.

Curiously, POs are of the same opinion regarding the value of the site investigation and its associated report:

Yeah, the investigation is important. You've got to do homework to prepare for a new client and the site investigation is the most important part of the homework. Now the report, well, that's just some red tape that those jerks downtown dreamed up to make life miserable for POs. I'll tell you how important the report is. I write them up in two minutes. I time myself. I start writing, and when two minutes are up, I sign whatever I've got down on paper. Nobody reads those things anyway.

The exaggeration not withstanding, this attitude is typical.

Finally, the statement of a branch officer supervisor illustrates the importance of the site investigation to certain routines: "I train my POs to be environmentalists. An environmentalist uses the parolee's environment as a tool. You'll see how that works when you go out in the field with my POs."

Branch office-supervisors ordinarily define the standards and methods of work for their POs. All supervisors demand that their POs conduct thorough site investigations for reasons that will be made apparent.

The role of the site investigation in the typing process may be stated generally in terms of *control*. POs are expected to control their parolees, and on the basis of the skeleton dossier, two parolees may appear to be equally controllable or uncontrollable. However, the parolees may be released to radically different environments, and consequently, may differ substantially in controllability. The difference is due entirely to facets of the environment that can be used as tools. This is what the PO looks for when he conducts a site investigation. Thus, on the basis of information found in the skeleton dossier, the PO may decide that a new parolee is a potential troublemaker. However, on the basis of the site investigation, the PO may decide that he can control the new parolee. As a consequence, the PO will type the new parolee differently.

THE INITIAL INTERVIEW

Sometimes the PO has doubts about his tentative typing decision. The initial interview with the new client can be used to clear these doubts up. In one case, for example, a PO told a

new parolee: "I've got your number, Ike. If you want to start a
new life with me, I'll let you. But if you want to buy trouble
from me, mister, that's cool too. I know all about you and I'll
be watching.

The new parolee appeared frightened by this unanticipated
attack. Later, the PO explained his behavior to me:

> I just wanted to see how far I could push him. That's an important
> thing to know about a new client. I didn't really hear anything bad
> about him. I made that up. If I'd heard any scuttlebutt on him, I
> wouldn't have tried him out like that. He was scared, so he won't be
> any trouble. But if he'd laughed at me, then I'd know to expect
> trouble. . . . Now what I'll do is I'll call him up tonight and apologize
> for losing my cool in there. He'll be relieved and then we'll be like
> two brothers. You watch. He'll be a good parolee.

Tests of this nature are used strictly to resolve doubts about the
new parolee's controllability.

SUBSEQUENT INTERACTION

The first three stages of the typing process are concerned
with "trouble." The PO uses the skeleton dossier, the site
investigation, and the initial interview to decide how much
"trouble" to expect from the new parolee. A certain number of
parolees are typed as "troublemakers" of one sort or another at
this point. Other parolees remain untyped. After a period of
interaction with these parolees, the PO may decide that some fit
into a particular category related to the roles they play in the
interaction. The most common role for the PO is "therapist" or
"counselor," and the PO will type some parolees as "counselable" on the basis of how well they play a role complementary
to his. Needless to say, this parolee-type is independent of the
PO's understanding of "trouble." The exception, of course, is
that a "troublemaker" will never be seen as "counselable."

TROUBLE

Three stages of the typing process are directly related to the
amount of "trouble" a PO expects from a new parolee. It is

important to note at this point that POs understand "trouble" in an idiosyncratic definition. For example, the County Prosecutor once asked a PO to obtain a copy of a parolee's income tax returns. The PO recognized the political implications of this request: "Auslander's a prick. I don't have the right to see that man's tax returns and Auslander doesn't either. That's why he didn't make the request in writing. All I can do is *ask* the man to give me a copy." When the PO asked his client for a copy of his income tax returns, the client refused. The parolee was thus judged a "troublemaker" because, by refusing to cooperate, he made his PO look ineffective.

The true meaning of "trouble" is seen in statements made by POs about individual clients. For example:

> Gangbangers cause me the most trouble. I personally don't care if the dude hangs out with a street gang. That's not necessarily a criminal thing. In some neighborhoods, every dude between ten and forty years old belongs [to a street gang]. But the trouble comes from the police. I get calls from the Gang Intelligence Unit saying that one of my dudes is a belonger. That makes it look like I'm not doing my job. What am I supposed to do? I can't revoke the dude unless he's in violation [of the parole contract] and hanging around on a street corner isn't a violation.

"Trouble" comes about as a result of moral judgments, usually on the part of some other criminal justice agency such as the Gang Intelligence Unit or the County Prosecutor. The PO is expected to enforce these moral judgments, and if he can do this, his image with these agencies is enhanced. Conversely, if he cannot enforce the moral judgments of others, his image suffers.

"Trouble" relates directly to control. If a PO can control his clients in an efficient manner, he eliminates "trouble." The following anecdote illustrates how a PO might control an otherwise uncontrollable client:

> A couple of years ago this happened. I got a call from the cops about one of my parolees. It seems the parolee was parking his car in front of a grocery store during the day. Well, there's nothing illegal about that, but this grocer had some clout and it looked like he could

make trouble for us. I called the parolee up and explained it to him
but he refused to cooperate. So I called his sister up and explained it
to her—exaggerated it a little bit, of course. The parolee never
parked his car there again. The moral of that story is, Don't ever
underestimate the rehabilitative power of a nagging sister.

POs typically exercise control over clients by such means. In
the next section, I will demonstrate exactly how the typing
process allows POs to control otherwise uncontrollable parolees.

Dangerous Men

Nearly every PO has one or two "dangerous men." As POs
use this term, it refers not to the parolee's innate propensity for
violence, as one might suspect, but rather, to the rationality or
predictability of the parolee's behavior. POs ordinarily control
their parolees with threats of punishment or promises of reward. A dangerous man does not respond rationally to threats
or promises, so the dangerous man cannot be controlled absolutely.

The quality of dangerousness varies along a continuum. At
one extreme is the so-called "tired dude" who responds well to
implied threats:

> You know Popeye, don't you? Well, he's what you call a tired dude.
> He just finished a seventeen-year stretch for murder and he doesn't
> want to go back. Most murderers are tired dudes because they done
> big time. You take Popeye. If I told him to jump, he'd ask me,
> "How high?" on the way up. A tired dude usually tells you right out
> front that he doesn't want any trouble.

The tired dude is cowed or broken. On the other extreme are
the truly dangerous men who do not respond at all to threats or
to any other contingencies or incentives at the PO's disposal:

> I'll tell you why he's dangerous. With most clients, a friendly
> warning is enough to straighten a problem out. Sometimes you have
> to go through the motions of writing an official warning. But that

doesn't even faze him. I don't understand clients like that. They're not living in the real world. They go out of their way to make trouble. They've got chips on their shoulders.

In a similar manner, POs try to control parolees by promising rewards for good behavior. One such reward is an early discharge from parole supervision:

Alright, Johnny, this is how it is. I've got you on paper for the next seven years but I'll make a deal with you. You give me two years of good behavior and I'll recommend you for early discharge. When I say 'good behavior,' though, I mean *cooperation*. When I tell you to do something, you do it. You don't argue with me about whether I'm right or wrong or whether it's fair or not, or even whether I have the right to tell you to do it. You just do it. If you give me two years of cooperation like that, I'll give you an early discharge.[3]

To most parolees, an early discharge is valuable. However, some parolees see little value in an early discharge for one reason or another. These parolees may be dangerous men.

A dangerous man ordinarily has items in his skeleton dossier suggesting that he is uncontrollable. For example, his behavior record in prison may have been poor. The PO nevertheless withholds his decision until after the site investigation is completed. During the site investigation, the PO will examine the new parolee's environment, looking for tools. The variety of environmental facets that can be used as tools is illustrated by this statement:

The family is important. You can use them as an intelligence source. Church affiliation is important too. You get the neighborhood clergyman involved in the case and you might have a powerful weapon. The client's job is important too. If he has a good job waiting for him, you have something you can really use. You can threaten to screw him up with his employer if he doesn't behave. If your client doesn't have a job, or worse, if he's got a shit-job, you don't have that weapon. Employment is very important to me. I always try to get my clients decent, good-paying jobs. That helps them and it also gives me more control.[4]

Thus, an item in the skeleton dossier may indicate that a new parolee is a potential troublemaker, or perhaps, even a dangerous man. However, after the site investigation, the PO may conclude the opposite. This switchabout reflects no change in the parolee's potential for trouble, but rather, a change in the PO's estimate of his ability to control the new parolee. Of course, control will usually be associated with some environmental facet.

Sometimes the PO will be undecided even after the site investigation is completed. The PO might then withhold his judgment until after his initial interview with the new parolee. It is interesting here to compare the attitudes of POs and higher DC administrators. A DC official told me:

A goodly percentage of parolees fail on their first day of freedom. They had no intention of living up to the parole contract, so they don't even go through the motions of reporting to their POs. Now as you know, one of our responsibilities is to protect the public, so it's important that we discover failures as soon as possible. By emphasizing the first meeting between PO and parolee, we're able to discover a great number of failures immediately.

The initial interview allows the bureaucracy to discover mistakes quickly, thereby minimizing certain costs. But POs see another value to the initial interview. It is the last chance to gather information for the typing process. If a PO is still unsure at this point, he may use the initial interview as a test. If the new parolee fails the test, he is typed as a dangerous man.

Concerning dangerousness, the PO typically forms an opinion on the basis of information in the skeleton dossier. Given that a parolee is a potential troublemaker, the PO will use the site investigation to estimate his ability to control the troublemaker. If the PO concludes that, first, the new parolee is a potential troublemaker, and second, that the new parolee cannot be easily controlled, the PO will decide that the new parolee is a dangerous man.

The utility of this decision is not obvious. By typing a new parolee as a dangerous man, the PO provokes a response at every level of the bureaucracy. A branch office supervisor explained:

> I'm ordinarily conservative about okaying sanctions against a parolee. The PO has to convince me that the sanction is absolutely necessary. Of course, if the parolee's dangerous, that's another story. I just tell my boss that the parolee's dangerous and the sanction gets expedited all the way up the line. There's limits to that, of course, I don't want my POs to use that cop-out too often. There just aren't that many dangerous men, and even if there were, my boss would question it.

Other supervisors agreed substantially with this statement, but sometimes stressing other aspects:

> POs have an advantage when they call a client dangerous. We usually don't okay parole revocations on technical grounds. The single exception to that is the case where the PO says, in writing, that the parolee is dangerous. In those cases, I countersign the revocation warrant without questioning the grounds. Now you have to realize that those are rare cases. If one of my POs came up with more than four or five dangerous parolees in a year, why, I think I'd bring the PO in here for a little chat. But that's never happened.

POs might be expected to overuse this label, minimizing Type II errors. When a PO announces to his supervisor that a new parolee is dangerous, however, the PO will be expected to set an intensive supervision schedule for the dangerous man. The PO increases his workload, so new parolees are judged dangerous only when the PO has exhausted less costly options.

The dangerous man label is actually committed to writing and POs are aware of the symbolic imagery. One PO related a germane anecdote:

> Remember the [famous] murder case. I'd just started here when that broke. His PO predicted that murder in the very first report he wrote. I saw the report. It said, "This subject is dangerous. His parole should be revoked at the first sign of trouble." Well, the DC didn't do anything about it. After the murder was discovered, some

reporters found that original report in the files and they made a big deal out of it. The DC learned its lesson from that. Now, if you write up a report like that, you get all the help you need. All it is is blackmail but they let you get away with it as long as you don't do it too often. I have maybe one or two parolees who give me a lot of trouble. I've got them typed as dangerous men, and the first time they violate parole, they're going back.

As it is used, the dangerous man label often amounts to symbolic overkill. The dangerous man is dangerous only to his PO, and then, only because the dangerous man is a troublemaker.

But the point here is that POs are expected to control their parolees in an absolute sense. When the PO has no other alternative, he resorts to that aspect of the typing process which enhances his ability to control the parolee. Naturally, typing a parolee as a dangerous man must be the last resort. In the next section, I will describe a parolee type that is functionally similar but that yet can be applied more indiscriminately.

Criminals

POs often speak of the noncriminals in their caseloads. The sense of this parolee type is: "Pete's not a criminal. He's a wino. Criminals don't have excuses for the things they do. Pete does. He has deep personal problems that cause him to do those things."

The noncriminal parolee types include "addicts," the vocationally or educationally "handicapped" parolee, and the "violent offender." Not coincidentally, the DC maintains special treatment programs for these parolee types. By implication, a criminal is any parolee who is ineligible for admission to one of these programs.

The criminal/noncriminal typing decision is made in the first stage of the typing process. When the PO reviews a skeleton dossier, he consciously tests the feasibility of various noncriminal typings:

The first thing I look for is drug related arrests on the rap sheet—or alcohol. You know what I mean. If the guy's got a couple of [public drunkenness] arrests, then I can make a pretty good case for transferring him to an alcoholic treatment program.... I wait a month or so to see if the guy's going to give me any trouble. If he's okay, I keep him. If he's a troublemaker, I write him up for a transfer.

After the transfer, the offending parolee is physically removed from the PO's caseload. A smooth transfer requires some evidence that the parolee is a noncriminal, however, and this evidence typically comes from the skeleton dossier.

Noncriminal typing options give the PO an opportunity to rid his caseload of potential troublemakers without invoking the costly dangerous man symbol. And POs are quite frank about their motives:

Listen, the DC judges us POs on the basis of how much trouble comes out of our caseloads. We'd be foolish not to take advantage of the [treatment programs].... That's not as cynical as it sounds. Take junkies, for example. Once a junkie, always a junkie. They can cause me a lot of trouble. You know, just bullshit trouble. Now why should I put up with that when I can get rid of my junkies through the [treatment programs]?... I'm not saying that I don't give junkies a chance to make it on my caseload. I give everybody a chance. But if I see a couple of [narcotic] busts on a rap sheet, I see that as a safety valve.

In a typical case, a PO notes the feasibility of a noncriminal label in his first report. Should the new parolee prove uncontrollable, this report facilitates the transfer of the parolee to a noncriminal treatment program. After transfer, the troublemaker is physically removed from the PO's caseload. Even when transfer is delayed, however, the noncriminal label relieves the PO of personal responsibility in the case. He is not expected to be able to control clients with "deep personal problems."

Noncriminal typing decisions illustrate how low level bureaucrats can adapt an otherwise legitimate typing scheme to accommodate operational problems. POs are faced with the problem of controlling parolees. When normal methods prove ineffective, the PO can solve his problem by making the appropriate typing decision. However, there are other interests here. Presumably, the treatment programs do not like troublemakers either, so treatment program personnel might be expected to resist typing decisions that appear expedient and arbitrary. For example, program personnel might devise their own criteria of admission, ignoring the typing decisions of POs. But as it turns out, there is another operational problem which coincides with the problem of controlling troublemakers.

Since the late 1960s, the DC has received substantial Federal funding for programs meant to treat certain parolee types. Refunding contingencies have created a set of informal demands within the bureaucracy. Referring to a specific treatment program, one DC official told me: "[The program] was badly needed but I imagine we would have applied for the grant anyway. We were able to expand our field staff by nearly 50 percent with that grant. Frankly, I don't know how we'll manage if [that program] isn't refunded next year."

To be refunded, a program must fulfill a specific need of the parolee population. On this point, the same DC official commented:

> The [funding agency] people try to maximize the number of service units delivered per dollar. To us, that means servicing as many parolees as possible without sacrificing quality. The underutilization problem we have right now is due to parolees leaving the program faster than they enter. That creates a surplus capacity which makes it look on paper like we really don't need the program. We're trying to alleviate the problem by cutting red tape. Right now it takes almost eight weeks from the time the PO starts his paperwork until the parolee actually enters the program.

These statements hint at the pressures on DC officials. The general policy of the DC is to make full use of treatment programs and this policy underlies the criminal/noncriminal typing process. POs who use these parolee types in their work are rewarded. POs who are unable or unwilling to type parolees as criminals or noncriminals are punished.

The policy transmission mechanism is typical of most informal mechanisms in the bureaucracy. Official policy starts at the top of the DC hierarchy and is first transmitted to the branch office supervisors. In late 1974, one supervisor related this incident to me:

> Barney took us [supervisors] out to lunch today to explain the new parole contract. They're trying to do away with the technical violations, I think. He wants us to keep a closer eye on the POs to make sure they're using the treatment programs as much as possible. A lot of technical violators should be handled as treatment cases instead.

The supervisors of other branch offices verified this incident substantially. All came away from the meeting with the impression that the DC wanted treatment programs to be emphasized.

In the months following this meeting, the supervisors began to stress treatment with their POs. Whenever a PO requested a revocation warrant on technical grounds, the supervisor sent the PO back into the field for "further investigation" of the case. POs soon discovered that it was easier to request a parolee "transferred for treatment." By doing this, POs eliminated the sure request for "further investigation" in the case. In other words, the POs cut down the amount of work they were required to do. Within six months, the number of formal and informal requests for revocation warrants had dropped substantially.

In one branch office, the supervisor held a meeting with his POs to discuss the new policy. According to a PO who attended this meeting:

> Matt wants us to start using the treatment programs more. That's not a problem with everybody. Some of us use the programs a lot already but some POs don't use them at all. He wants us to start going through our caseloads to look for treatable clients. . . . There's no quota or anything like that. He just wants us to start thinking about the treatment programs more. . . . Well, he said that if we don't start sending more clients to the programs, the DC might send auditors into our office to find out why. Nobody wants auditors going through the files. That causes trouble.

To avoid trouble, POs quickly adjusted to the new typing scheme.

Typing parolees as criminals or noncriminals seems rationally justified. One of the parole agency's legitimate goals is rehabilitation and the typing scheme assures that parolees who are amenable to rehabilitation will receive the necessary services. However, the original thesis is that the typing scheme may be adapted to accommodate operational problems. In this case, POs had the problem of controlling potential troublemakers. DC administrators, who might otherwise be expected to monitor typing decisions, also had a problem. The volume of treatment had to be inflated in order to secure operating funds for the bureaucracy. The noncriminal typing scheme was well suited to both problems, and consequently, the rationality of the typing scheme suffered.

Sincere Clients

The notion of sincerity refers in a general way to a parolee's internalized motivation. In one sense, the PO's goal is to rehabilitate the parolee and a sincere client is one who shares this goal for its sake alone. Obviously, a sincere client never causes trouble and he cooperates with his PO when trouble arises from another source. Although many POs use this term and classification scheme routinely, only a few have a conscious idea of its meaning:

> A sincere client comes to me with his problems. He doesn't hold anything back. A sincere client's honest too. Some of these bums even lie to me about where they live. Most of them don't want my help anyway. I'm not going to chase a client around and kiss his ass. When a client's in trouble, I expect him to tell me about it—and not after it's too late to do anything. . . . It's more complicated than that, but I can't explain it. It's just a feeling you get from working with a particular client. You know what I mean. He's *sincere*.

Many POs use the term to refer to special parolees. Sincerity has a technical meaning, however. It refers directly to the parolee's willingness to accept his PO as a counselor or therapist. In one branch office, for example, two POs set up a series of informal group therapy sessions. The POs told their officemates:

> We're only interested in your sincere clients for the groups. No talkers or programmers. We think we can get fifteen clients right away, so we're scheduling two groups as a start. When we get more clients, we'll start another group. Now remember, we only want your sincere clients. The therapy won't work otherwise.

A "talker" is a neurotic parolee who, if encouraged, will monopolize his PO's time. A "programmer" is an insincere client who feigns sincerity, usually to impress his PO, sometimes to "rip off" the PO.[5] The fact that most POs recognize and can use these terms correctly indicates that POs do think of parolees in terms of counselability. Of course, this is a function of how closely the PO identifies himself as a counselor or therapist.

The decision that a given parolee is sincere comes in the middle of the parole experience. A PO may have decided, for example, that the parolee is not a criminal, or if he is, that the parolee can be controlled. At some later time, the PO may also decide that the parolee is sincere. The PO will then begin to counsel the parolee, and the parolee in turn will begin to assume the role of client. The sincere client becomes a special parolee. PO and parolee will interact frequently and informally.

On the other hand, the PO may have decided that a given parolee is a criminal, and worse, that the parolee cannot be controlled. The PO is likely to decide that this parolee is a dangerous man, and of course, dangerous men can never become serious clients. Or alternatively, the PO may have decided that the parolee is not a criminal, or if he is, that the parolee can be controlled. This parolee would never be considered a dangerous man. The PO may nevertheless decide that this parolee is not a sincere client. PO and parolee will then interact infrequently and formally. Whereas a PO may see his sincere clients (and his dangerous men!) weekly, he will see the remainder of his caseload perhaps only one time in six months.

Sincerity is synonymous with counselability in one sense only. There is no absolute criterion shared by all POs. Instead, parolees are judged to be sincere or not by a nearly stochastic decision-making process. Sincere clients then are counselable only because, from the pool of all potentially counselable parolees, the PO has chosen these few. Each decision must be explained in case-specific terms and these make no sociological sense.

The importance of sincerity as a typing criterion is not universal. It is certainly more important to POs than to supervisors or administrators. Younger POs have degrees in a social science or in social work; most took jobs with the DC because of promised opportunities for counseling work. On the job, however, novice POs immediately discover that "paperwork is more important than peoplework." Yet because POs can organize their jobs around individual tastes, many are able to manufacture counseling opportunities. These opportunities usually consist of regular "rap sessions" with a few sincere clients, although POs have actually organized informal group therapy sessions in some of the branch offices. These counseling opportunities, and the interaction with sincere clients, are important to the PO. They are of lesser importance to supervisors and administrators, however.

The branch office supervisors neither discourage nor encourage their POs to counsel. In general, the supervisors do not appreciate sincere clients:

> If one of my POs tells me that a client is sincere, that means that the PO trusts this particular client. That's all it means and the importance of that is going to change depending upon who the PO is. Now it's an important thing to the PO because, frankly, you get personal satisfaction out of helping a sincere client. But I'm interested in more routine things at this level, so of course, I'm not interested in whether one of my POs *enjoys* working with a particular client.

At best, the supervisors, who were all POs themselves at one time, are only indifferent to sincere clients.[6] DC officials, in contrast, are incensed by the very notion of sincerity: "No parolee is uncounselable. I would agree that *some* POs have little success counseling *some* parolees. That's obvious. But this is the fault of the PO, not the parolee." The conventional response from DC administrators is that all parolees are counselable but that POs differ in counseling aptitudes; some POs have no aptitude for counseling whatsoever.

What is immediately interesting here is that the more contact an actor has with parolees, the more likely he is to appreciate sincere clients. POs, who regularly interact with parolees, think that sincerity is one of the most important typing criteria. Every PO knows who the sincere clients in his caseload are. Supervisors, who were once POs but who now interact with parolees only vicariously, tend to downplay the importance of sincerity as a typing criterion. And DC officials, who never interact with parolees, see sincerity as a bogus issue, a parolee characteristic that POs have invented to mask their lack of aptitude.

This relationship between interaction-with-parolees and attitudes-towards-sincerity is not surprising. The typing criterion described previously are used to accommodate certain routine problems. By deciding that a parolee is a dangerous man, for example, the PO solves a one-shot problem. Yet when the PO decides that a client is sincere, he solves a problem that is invisible to the administrators. Of course, the problem is *alienation,* and moreover, a type of alienation that arises from the conflict between idealistic "peoplework" and boring, realistic "paperwork."

Finally, there is some reason to believe that DC officials see sincerity as a threat to the bureaucratic status quo. DC officials have often remarked that an *in*competent PO is one who has grown too close to his parolees. DC officials fear that, when a PO overidentifies with his caseload, the PO will no longer be able to impersonally enforce DC policy. Of course, this is true. Not only does a PO not enforce punitive DC policies in the cases of his sincere clients, the PO may explicitly break rules and regulations to their benefit.

Eisenstadt (1959; Eisenstadt and Katz, 1960) names the general process whereby clients co-opt the bureaucratic worker, "debureaucratization." In most service bureaucracies, it is assumed that all workers who routinely interact with clients are debureaucratized to some extent or another. We see that this is not the case with POs, however. The PO is debureaucratized only with respect to his sincere clients. This differential effect may be due strictly to the quantity and quality of the PO's interaction with his clients. Most parolees avoid their POs. A sincere client, on the other hand, seeks out his PO and interacts with him frequently. Moreover, the quality of the interaction is high. Of all those parolees who seek out the PO, the PO chooses only the brightest, most pleasant, and most honest as his sincere clients. Counseling these sincere clients gives the POs great satisfaction, but as a result, it is likely that these sincere clients have co-opted or socialized the PO.

On Becoming a Client

Figure 4.1 shows the four-stage typing process, mapped as a series of successive decisions and associated types. The first two decisions lead to *temporary* type-states: noncriminals and controllables. The second two decisions lead to *permanent* type-states: dangerous men, clients, and paper men. I will have more to say about paper men shortly.

When a prisoner receives a favorable verdict from the parole board, a skeleton dossier is forwarded to a branch office. The branch office supervisor assigns the skeleton dossier to a PO on the basis of the new parolee's address. The PO then reviews the skeleton dossier and makes a crucial decision: Is the new parolee a criminal? If the new parolee is not a criminal, the decision-making process comes to a halt. The PO has discovered a safety valve in the case, so no further decisions are needed. Should the new parolee turn out to be a troublemaker, the PO can easily blame the trouble on a pathological condition. By doing this, the PO relieves himself of the personal responsibility for controlling the parolee and also rids himself of the troublemaker. The new parolee will be transferred to a special treatment caseload.

But if the new parolee *is* a criminal, the PO is required to make another decision: Is the new parolee controllable? During

Figure 4.1: The Decision-Making Process

(1) The skelton dossier
Is the parolee any one of the noncriminal types? If so, the PO has a safety valve in the case. The decision-making process skips to the fourth stage.

(2) The site investigation
The parolee is a criminal. Can environmental facets (e.g., job, family, etc.) be used to control the parolee? If so, the decision-making process skips to the fourth stage.

(3) The initial interview
The PO must decide at this time whether the parolee is a dangerous man. If he is, the decision-making process stops.

(4) Subsequent interaction
Is the parolee sincere? If so, the PO assumes the role of a therapist, the parolee assumes the role of a client.

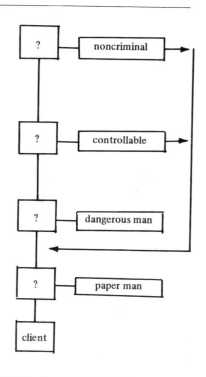

the site investigation, the PO searches the new parolee's environment for tools. A good job or family, if the parolee has either, can be used to control an otherwise uncontrollable parolee. In many cases, where no tools exist, the PO can build them into the environment. The PO might try to obtain lucrative employment for the parolee, for example, or if the new parolee appears to have the requisite ability and credentials, the PO might try to arrange some attractive program such as educational or vocational training. Once the new parolee commits himself to such a program, he becomes controllable. If trouble comes up, the PO can threaten to terminate the arrangement.

But sometimes a new parolee is a criminal, and as far as the PO can tell, uncontrollable. The PO must then consider the possibility that the parolee is a dangerous man. The PO will not take this decision lightly because he pays a price for invoking the dangerous man label. The PO *must* control each and every one of his parolees, so if a new parolee is indeed dangerous, the PO will say so. However, due to the steep price, the PO will invoke this label only as a last resort. Quite often, the PO holds up on the decision until after his first meeting with the new parolee. Note, however, that the decision can be made no later than this time. The DC expects POs to control parolees, or if not, to announce that a parolee is uncontrollable. But once the PO accepts a parolee into his caseload, the DC will accept no excuses. Unless the PO speaks up at the very beginning of the parole experience, he certifies that the new parolee is *not* a dangerous man. Any trouble after that time is attributed to the PO, not to the parolee.

A good percentage of all new parolees are not criminals.[7] In addition, the majority of new parolees who are criminals can be controlled, so the PO expects no trouble at all from the bulk of his caseload. When trouble arises, the PO handles it quickly with threats or promises, or in the case of some noncriminals, by getting rid of the troublemaker. The few dangerous men are watched closely and returned to prison at the first oppor-tunity.[8]

After a short period of adjustment, usually no more than a month, the PO and his new parolee settle into a period of routine interaction. During this period, the PO may decide that the new parolee is sincere. This decision is the fourth stage of the typing process shown in Figure 4.1. From another perspec-tive, the four stages of the decision-making process depict the process of becoming a client. Should the PO decide that a new parolee is sincere, the parolee is transformed into a *client*. As a client, the parolee plays a role complementary to his PO-coun-selor. The pair interact frequently in this role context. Most important, when a parolee becomes a client, he becomes a special parolee and the outcome of his parole is assured. Should he slip or stumble at some point during the parole experience, he counts on his PO to "save" him.

The alternative to becoming a client is to become a paper man. These parolees are all those who have been judged *in*sincere, but nevertheless controllable, and all those who have not been judged at all. In an average caseload, no more than a dozen parolees are dangerous men or clients. All the rest are paper men. Whereas the interaction between PO and the dangerous man can be characterized as *surveillance,* and the interaction between PO and client as *counseling,* the interaction between PO and paper man must be characterized as mutual disinterested toleration. The PO sees his dangerous men and clients nearly every week. He sees his paper men only one or two times in a year.

The term *paper* man comes from the phrase "on paper" which POs use as a synonym for "on parole." There is a subtle secondary meaning to this phrase, however. Once I asked one PO how he was able to handle his extremely large caseload. He told me:

> Well, that's how many men I've got *on paper.* Actually, I've only got about a dozen men that I worry about. I spend a lot of time with my men the first week they're out of the joint. If they look like they're doing okay, I don't bother them anymore. I only see most of my men two or three times a year. But they're still *on paper.*

And this is the kernel of the parole experience. Professors might see an analogy to the large lecture course. Of the hundred or more students registered for the course, there are no more than a dozen who interact personally with the professor. These are the dullest and brightest students. The remainder, the faceless majority, are paper students.

Finally, the typing scheme in practice reduces to the decisionmaking process outline in Figure 4.1. Typing decisions are made by POs, and as there is no simple method to evaluate these decisions, POs are encouraged to use the scheme in a way that accommodates routine problems. These have little bearing on the legitimate goals of the bureaucracy or on the justification for typing parolees. The typing scheme thus can be rationally justified only to the extent that the motives of POs coincide with the legitimate goals of the DC.

NOTES

1. According to the civil service code, POs are "parole counselors."

2. See Heinz et al. (1977) for a discussion of these assessments. The prison social workers operate under career contingencies similar to those described for POs. Not surprisingly, record writing phenomena, as described in Chapter 5, are similar.

3. Cases are reviewed annually. If a PO keeps a parolee on paper longer than two years, he must justify his decision. Parolees thus are discharged almost automatically after two years of supervision. Most are unaware of this policy, however. The promise of an early discharge is consequently effective. Most parolees think they are receiving something of great value.

4. This is a fine example of doing the right thing for the wrong reason. The POs take great pains to set their new parolees up in "good" jobs. The PO's motive relates strictly to control.

5. The term "programmer" is commonly heard in prisons, referring to prisoners who volunteer for "treatment programs" in order to impress the parole board. With the exception of these POs, I have never heard the term used to describe analogous parolee behavior.

6. Two points. First, none of the supervisors have college degrees, so none appreciate sincerity to the full extent. Second, when a PO tells his supervisor that a client is sincere, this might suggest to the supervisor that the PO should be watched closely. This is especially true of incompetent and novice POs. As detailed in Chapter 3, the supervisor might expect trouble in such a case.

7. Remember that caseloads are geographically defined, and hence, variable. Some caseloads are all-white, some all-black, and some all-Spanish, for example. However, no caseload would have fewer than 30 percent noncriminal parolees or more than 70 percent. This reflects the great number of special treatment caseloads available.

8. From 1975 to the present, I tracked thirteen dangerous men through the criminal justice system. Due to access problems, this does not reflect the total number. Of the thirteen, ten were returned to prison for new crimes and/or parole violations; two died while on parole, one from gunshot wounds; the thirteenth dangerous man was discharged from parole after winning a series of lawsuits.

Chapter 5

PAPERWORK[1]

A parole bureaucracy uses its records to classify and process men released from prison. Assuming only this internal use, ideal parole records should give an accurate description of parolee behavior according to the classification criteria. In fact, however, parole records are more likely to reflect the needs and problems of POs. This bureaucratic dysfunction can be attributed to the great discretion allowed POs in the gathering and reporting of information. In most cases, the PO himself decides what portion of the information he has gathered will actually go into the official record. By exercising editorial discretion in this area, the PO can suppress information that might make his job more difficult or complex and can include information that might facilitate work goals or objectives. This is how POs "use" their records.

Traditional studies of the PO's work environment have divided it into two distinct halves, the PO-parolee interaction and the PO-bureaucracy interaction. Glaser's (1964; See also Irwin, 1970) view of the PO-parolee interaction is typical in that it emphasizes control; a successful PO is one who can control his clients. Takagi (1967) has noted that within this context, a successful PO must also balance and satisfy certain explicit and implicit demands of the bureaucracy. The factor common to these two halves of the PO's work environment is record-keeping and a successful PO is one who knows how to "use" his records. As it turns out, this is not a simple task. Straightforward record-keeping entails real costs that the PO must weigh against the potential benefit realized from "using" his records.

This chapter begins with a note on the unique historical determinants of record-keeping in the parole bureaucracy. The practical costs of record-keeping are then outlined in detail. My argument here is based on a claim that, *ceteris paribus*, a PO will not report any of the minor crimes, incidents, or violations he observes in his caseload. When a PO does report an incident, he is creating records that will accomplish some end, the benefits of which are expected to outweigh the practical costs of reporting the incident. The implication of this argument is that parole records do not accurately reflect the behavior of parolees, but rather, reflect the many problems that arise in the PO's work environment. Three general problems to be discussed here lead to the three most common "uses" of records: (1) records created to threaten parolees, (2) records created to get rid of troublesome parolees, and (3) records created to protect the PO and his superiors.

History

Many of the phenomena described here are due to recent changes in the law, particularly the U.S. Supreme Court decision in *Morrissey versus Brewer* which extended the Constitutional protection of due process to parolees. Prior to 1971, a PO could detain a parolee in county jail for weeks without filing any actual charges; parolees could be returned to prison on the basis of the PO's determination that the parolee had a "bad attitude" or was making a "poor adjustment to parole." After 1971, POs were required for the first time to file specific charges before ordering a parolee detained. Furthermore, parolees were given the right to a quasi-judicial hearing on all charges the PO might file. The parolee or his attorney had the right to cross-examine the complaining PO in this hearing and the decision or verdict of the hearing could be appealed to the courts. The effects of *Morrissey* on the PO's work environment were traumatic. To begin with, POs lost much of their strategic advantage in the PO-parolee interaction. Because charges were required to be specific and provable in hearing, it became difficult to reimprison parolees on the basis of subjective catch-all charges such as "bad attitude." Post-*Morrissey*, POs could no longer control their parolees in an absolute sense.

But more importantly, *Morrissey* introduced a new set of bureaucratic demands. Before 1971, the bureaucracy used its records internally to classify and process men released from prison. After 1971, the bureaucracy began more and more to use its records externally to justify classification decisions to outside agencies, such as the courts. It was only after 1971, for example, that the DC began to use electronic data processing equipment for cataloging and retrieving parole records. This abrupt change had the effect of introducing accountability and decision costs into the PO's work environment. One veteran PO described the change this way:

> It used to be 'the' records, now it's 'my' records. If I recall correctly, in the old days, I never signed my monthly reports. If I forget to sign one now, Terry sends it back to me. Nothing gets out of this (branch) office without a signature. That's so they know who to come back to if there's any trouble.

After *Morrissey*, the DC was held accountable for its "bad" decisions. The DC in turn passed these costs on to the PO, so that now, whenever the PO initiates a record, he faces potentially consequential costs.

Routine Organization: Incentives for Underreporting

As far as the DC is concerned, a PO has two major duties. First, the PO must survey, and if necessary, service a given number of parolees. Surveillance and servicing are not well defined. As a rule of thumb, however, the DC would expect a PO to "know what's going on" in his caseload.

The PO's second major duty is to write such records as the DC requires to discharge its statutory obligations. Most of the records that a PO writes will consist of monthly reports. A PO must contact each of his parolees at least once in every month. In theory, any new information the PO gleans from these contacts will appear in the monthly reports, but in practice, this is seldom the case.

When things are going smoothly between a PO and his parolees, the monthly reports are dull and uneventful, containing little or no information. Reports are submitted to the branch office supervisor who approves them with his signature and forwards them to the DC. At the end of a month, the supervisor receives a computerized summary of all the records written by his POs. The summary serves as a ledger, telling the supervisor how many reports his POs owed for that month and how many reports they remitted. If a PO has somehow neglected to file a report on one of his parolees, the overdue report will be highlighted in the summary. When things are going smoothly then, the monthly reports are used only as a minimal check on the PO's job performance.

When things are not going smoothly between a PO and his parolees, the monthly reports will contain information relating to a crime, incident, or violation of the parole contract. The PO sometimes receives this information from another criminal justice agency and thus acts as a simple information conduit. More commonly, however, the PO discovers crimes, incidents, or violations on his own. While the PO is legally bound to report this information, practical considerations usually work in the other direction. These practical considerations, generating incentives for underreporting, fall into five major categories of cost.

(1) *Full reporting cuts into the PO's "free" time.* When asked what facet of their jobs is the most attractive, POs invariably mention the flexible schedule. For example:

My wife and I have a restaurant and this job gives me a lot of free time for the business. I spend two half-days a week here and then take care of my fieldwork in the evenings. When you have an arrangement like I have, you have to handle things off the record. If the cops catch one of my men shooting up, I go through the motions of requesting a warrant. But if I catch the man myself, I handle it my own way. My way accomplishes the same thing and only takes one tenth the time. I've got my own style. If I went by the book, they'd have me down here six days a week writing reports.

Half the POs on this side of town are full-time students. This job doesn't pay much and it doesn't offer much of a future. But if you're going to school, it's perfect because the hours aren't set. If I can do my job in twenty hours, that's my business.

Most POs moonlight at other pursuits that require a flexible schedule. In general, underreporting crimes, incidents, and violations will maximize the PO's "free" time.[2]

(2) *Full reporting places the PO in jeopardy.* Whenever the PO reports an incident, he runs the risk of a hearing. A DC superior reading the report may pressure the PO to request a warrant. The warrant must go to hearing, and as POs see it, this is a risk:

When you go into that hearing, you're the one on trial. . . . If you lose the hearing, the DC people never let you forget it. They don't tell you up front, but they expect you to perjure yourself if the hearing gets close. I won't do that. I'll tell you how ridiculous it is. When I catch a parolee in violation, I handle it myself. If I reported it, somebody would get after me to file a warrant and I don't need that headache.

POs routinely speak of "winning" or "losing" revocation hearings. During the course of this study, nearly all revocation warrants were based on information developed by the police or prosecutor, not on information developed by POs. While this trend permits a number of plausible interpretations, it is fully consistent with the claim made here: POs ignore minor crimes, incidents, and violations that they might be required to "prove" in hearings.

(3) *POs believe that the DC evaluates their performance on the basis of their caseload return-to-prison rates.* An incident becomes actionable only after the PO reports it. Thus, the more crimes, incidents, or violations the PO reports, the higher will be his return-to-prison statistic. On this point, a branch office supervisor made this revealing comment:

> New POs always ask me how many revocations the DC wants them to have in a year. I always answer that we don't have quotas but I don't think they believe me. It's funny the way they ask too—like it's a company secret. Then they go away mad because I won't trust them with the secret number. . . . Most POs have a quota mentality of some sort.

This supervisor's impression is accurate. POs place a great emphasis on their caseload return statistic:

> I don't think it's a secret around here that the POs with the lowest return rates get all the goodies. . . . I have the lowest return rate in this office and it generates a lot of malice. . . . No, I don't try to meet a quota. It's simply a result of my work style. I'm effective.
>
> The quickest way to get your books audited is to come up with too many revocations. I've seen that happen to a lot of POs.

There are no data to suggest that the DC evaluates its POs on the basis of this or any other statistic.[3] Nevertheless, a majority of POs operate under a "quota mentality" that leads to underreporting.

(4) *Full reporting may result in "busy work" for the PO.* To a PO, much of the work assigned by his supervisor is considered to be "busy work," that is, work that is not only time consuming but also unnecessary. In fact, a supervisor can punish a PO informally by creating "busy work." How this factor leads to underreporting is illustrated in the special case of missing or AWOL parolees. A supervisor described the general situation this way:

> When a PO can't find a parolee, he submits an AWOL report. Thirty days later, the DC issues an apprehension warrant. When the parolee

is apprehended, he gets a hearing and is sent back to prison. Of course, it's not that cut and dried. For one thing, I suspect that many of my POs make informal arrangements with their parolees. So if one of my POs comes in here with an AWOL report, I want him to be damn sure that the parolee's not attending his mother's funeral or something like that. The parolee might have thought that his PO didn't care about leaving the district for that sort of thing. Also, it's well known that POs have tricked their parolees into violation by giving them verbal permission to leave the district. I believe that's called 'bagging a man.' Well, sir, those things don't happen in my office because I make it difficult for my POs to file an AWOL report. I require a great deal of hard work before I [counter] sign one. In that way, I can satisfy myself that a report is basically honest and that it will stand up in hearing.

So in most cases, POs will not promptly report AWOL parolees: "You got to be stupid to report a dude AWOL. That's a lot of work. If you wait a few weeks, the dude will probably show up with some jive excuse. Otherwise he'll get busted ripping off. Either way, you saved yourself a lot of trouble by not reporting the dude AWOL."

AWOL parolees must be covered up. The methods range from Machiavellian deception to simple literary ambiguity, but whatever the method, it is usually easier for the PO to cover up the AWOL than to report it.

(5) *A PO may restrict his options by reporting a violation.* Some POs have stated explicitly that reporting incidents is not part of their "real" job: "It's not part of my job to catch clients in violation. When I do, I want to counsel the client and I can't do that if I work through the system. Once I report a violation, I lose my freedom to act as a professional."

This attitude is typical of the POs who view themselves as counselors or therapists. In a more general sense, reporting a violation restricts such options as "giving the man a second chance" or "giving a break" to a client who is deemed worthy: "What a PO can do is dispense justice. The system can't do that because of the regulations. When I see a client who deserves a break, I can give it to him as long as no one knows about it. I like helping parolees and sometimes that's the only way I can help." Most POs value this discretionary power greatly and thus underreport incidents for this reason alone.

These five specific cost categories can be generalized to time, effort, freedom, and jeopardy. Generally, whenever the PO reports an incident that he has discovered in his caseload, he risks paying a practical cost in terms of one or more of these items. Consequently, the PO will not report an incident unless the resulting record is practically useful to him in some way, that is, unless the potential benefits of recording the incident outweigh the potential costs. Underreporting then is the expected mode of behavior, reinforced by the organizational contingencies as outlined. I will now describe three general sets of circumstances under which POs will be inclined to break away from the expected mode. These circumstances create a counterbalancing incentive in that, by reporting an incident, the PO has created a useful record. The circumstances include situations where the PO can (1) initiate a record to threaten or coerce a parolee, (2) initiate a record to get rid of a troublesome parolee, or (3) initiate a record that will protect himself and his DC superiors.

Using Records to Threaten a Parolee

The first incentive for reporting an incident arises from the contingencies of supervising particular parolees. When things are not going smoothly between the PO and one of his clients, the fault may be with the PO, the DC, or with some outside agency. But if the parolee is at fault, that is, if the problem came about because of something the parolee has done or has not done, the PO can use his records to threaten, persuade, or coerce his client "back into line." The alternative mechanism of control, returning the troublesome client to prison, entails the risk of a warrant hearing.

To understand this phenomenon, consider what an official record or document means to the parolee. Throughout his prison career, social workers and security personnel thumbed through dossiers while making decisions that affected the inmate's life. Institutional assignments, assignments to rehabilitative programs, privileges, punishments, and eventually, even parole itself were all decided on the basis of papers kept in a manila folder. In the end, this ominous dossier follows the inmate out of prison.

During a group therapy session, a parolee described a routine visit to see his PO. The parolee's description of this episode is revealing:

> I go in to see him and he's acting real funny. You know, like I done something—but I didn't. I'm clean now. He asked me some real funny questions about my job, like how I was getting along with my boss and how I liked the work. Every time I answered a question, he looked in my file to see if I was telling the truth. I think he had a snitch sheet on me. I hope I answered all the questions right.

The reader will see comic possibilities in this (apparently) neurotic parolee's description of the episode. Most likely, the PO was initiating a friendly, off-the-record conversation during which he absent-mindedly picked up a dossier and began to page through it.

Yet the parolee's interpretation of this episode has a basis in fact that the naive reader will not suspect. Experienced POs are sensitive to the threatening aspects of dossiers and usually take some precautions to put their clients at ease. For example, I observed one PO writing a report in the presence of a client. The PO showed his client both the standardized form and an official document referred to in the report. The PO explained what each was and then asked the parolee if he had any questions. The PO later told me:

> I try not to do any writing while the man's in my office. If I have to, I always explain what I'm writing and why I have to write it. I show the man all the forms I have to use. This may sound funny, but a lot of parolees are like rabbits. They scare easily. I don't want a man to do something rash because he misunderstands something I'm doing. When I say "something rash," of course, I mean absconding.

This behavior is typical. Most POs will show clients routine documents to put the client at ease. For the same reason, most POs will answer any simple questions a client might ask about his dossier. But no PO would "absent-mindedly" page through a dossier in the presence of a client. This action has only one unambiguous meaning to the PO and to the parolee.

Just as a PO can physically manipulate files to intimidate, or alternatively, to relax a parolee, a PO may write reports under certain conditions for no other reason but intimidation.

The effects of the 1971 *Morrissey* decision must be reemphasized here. Before *Morrissey*, the PO was able to back up his threats in a very tangible way. One veteran PO described this situation:

> In the old days, you'd give a man a warning. If he didn't listen to you, you'd issue a "detain for investigation" warrant. He'd sit in jail for a few weeks while you "investigated," and believe me, that did the trick usually. Of course, if it didn't, well, then you had to send the man back to the joint. But at least you gave him two chances first. Nowadays you either ignore the violation or you send the man back to the joint. There's no in-betweens.

The difference is that the PO can no longer back his threats up swiftly and surely. This restructuring of the PO-parolee interaction has led directly to a number of novel ways to "use" records. This statement of a younger PO gives an intuitive notion of how clients can be threatened:

> In an average case, I'd start by giving the client a friendly warning. If that didn't work, I'd write an official warning. If the official warning didn't work, I'd try to place the client in a special caseload where he could receive individualized treatment. If there were no individualized treatment available, I might request a warrant. Then I'd try to reason with the client, and if we could work something out, I'd drop the warrant. If not, I'd still get one more chance to work something out at the hearing. One possibility might be an order that increased my revocation powers. Now that's about a half-dozen steps, right? It's a six-step escalation that I can stop at any time. What it does is it puts psychological pressure on the client. It shifts the burden of revocation back to him. He's forced to grow up or go back to jail.

The process amounts to a war of nerves between the PO and his client, each trying to dominate the other. Of course, the process was less necessary when POs had more effective weapons at their disposal.

The six-step escalation process has a number of by-product records, one of which is the "final, official warning." One PO described that record this way:

> These guys are misleading you with their talk about official warnings. There's no such thing. It's something they made up. I'll tell you what they mean. When you write the report, you say, "Gave client warning about such-and-such." Then you show that to the client to scare him. But it doesn't mean anything. If you really want to scare him, you send him his official warning by mail. One time I had this junkie—a white kid. His mother was causing problems for him. She didn't have any respect for me or for the job I was trying to do. Well, I finally gave him an official warning and mailed a copy to his mother. I never had any trouble with him after that. His mother kicked his ass every time he got out of line. But an official warning isn't *official.* The DC won't take any action on it. It's just something you use to bring a client back into line.

This PO was not entirely correct. Official warnings do have other uses:

> Of course, if you warn a man about something, and later on if it goes to revocation, you've protected yourself. The Public Defender is going to question your charges. So what you do is go back in your files and bring out the warning. The fact that the man didn't raise any objections at that time means that he's admitting to the basics of the warning, and by implication, the basics of the charge against him. So warnings have two uses. They let a man know you mean business—put the fear of God into him—and they protect you if you have to go after a warrant.

The revocation process itself has become largely a psychological weapon. A warrant will usually not be issued for a single violation complaint, but even if issued, it is not likely to be upheld in hearing. Warrants are still effective if used properly, however:

The trick to requesting warrants is finesse. You've got to rely on your reputation [with the supervisor] to get a warrant in the first place and then you've got to rely on your wits so it doesn't blow up in your face. A warrant is only good if you *don't* use it. Let me explain that. One time this dude cuts out to St. Louis to visit his family. I forgot where his family lived, so I reported him AWOL. When he got back to town, there was a warrant out on him. Now that was just sloppy work on my part. The warrant would have been thrown out in hearing and I would have looked like a chump. I think I gave him permission to cut out but then forgot to write it down. I should have called his mother before reporting him AWOL anyway. Well, I visited this dude in jail and told him I'd drop the warrant if he stayed out of trouble. The dude was so grateful that he broke down and cried. Later it occurred to me that that's the only way to use a warrant. The dude's got to be ignorant. You get a jailhouse lawyer or some smart gangbanger and he's going to laugh right in your face. Those dudes are too tough to scare. But if you've got a tired dude or a scared dude, you can break him with a warrant.

Revocation warrants can thus be "used" most effectively when the PO wants only to threaten a client.

The PO's motives in this connection are obvious. In Chapter 3, the concepts of *competence* and *realism* implied a certain amount of control; a competent, realistic PO appears to control his clients. Formal or official methods of control can be costly to the PO, however, while informal methods, which are often just as effective, may be less costly. Moreover, as the cost of formal control is born by the bureaucracy itself, the informal methods such as "using" records have become an accepted mode of operation. This is apparent in the typical comment of a branch office supervisor:

There's something final about the written word. A PO can talk himself blue in the face and get no response from the parolee. If he puts it down on paper, though, he gets results. Parolees know that once something gets written down, it's final. I encourage my POs to utilize their reports that way.

So, in general, a PO ignores incidents to minimize his risk and costs. But the DC expects the PO to control his parolees and

POs will report incidents then as a means to establish or reassert control over troublesome parolees.

Using Records to Get Rid of a Parolee

What is the PO to do when threats prove ineffective? Psychological coercion is always the preferred means of control; reimprisonment, as the potentially most costly alternative, is the least preferred. One option, lying midway between these two extremes, is to get rid of the troublesome parolee by reporting incidents that suggest some "treatable" pathology. The DC maintains a number of special programs to provide services for unusual parolee types. To place a client in one of these programs, the PO must first report one or more incidents in support of a pathological theory. These reports can serve double duty as threats. The PO, for example, can give the client a "final, official warning" about some pathological behavior. If the threat works, the PO has accomplished his goal. If not, the PO applies for an administrative order which will transfer the troublesome client out of the caseload and into a special program. The administrative order must be approved by the PO's supervisor, and often, by higher DC officials. As this procedure amounts to a good deal of extra work for the PO, the motivating circumstances must be strong.

In one case I observed, a parolee was accused of beating his wife. The police were called but took no action because the wife refused to make an official complaint. The police notified the DC, however, and the PO in charge of the case was asked to investigate the situation: "There wasn't too much to report. She didn't have any bruises, so it couldn't have been too bad. I think she just gets hysterical and goes overboard. There's nothing I can do in this case except warn the man and hope it doesn't happen again." But it did happen again, and as before, the wife refused to make an official complaint. This time the PO was reprimanded for his "inaction."

> I don't know what they want me to do. She doesn't have any marks on her and she won't press a charge. He denies even touching her. If

I went after a revocation on this, they'd throw it out and accuse me of overreacting. They want me to do something but they won't tell me what. If this happens again and she gets hurt or something, they're going to blame me for it.

The PO resolved this problem by transferring the parolee to a special treatment caseload for "violent offenders." But the PO was candid about his motives: "I felt like a fool arguing that he was violent. Violence had nothing to do with what was going on there. And I don't think the violent offender PO will be able to help. But it's not my problem now. I'm just happy to get rid of that case."

This case was unusual in a number of respects. The PO was a novice, and because he had not commented on his client's "violent" nature before this incident, the transfer was not as smooth as it might have been. Experienced POs will usually get rid of a case before the situation gets this far out of hand.

The general attitude among POs is that the special treatment programs are an *alternative* to reimprisonment. This statement is typical:

> In most cases, I'm going to have more freedom if my client is an addict. The reason for that is that we know how to deal with the problem. We've got special programs for addicts. If you take some other client whose problem is just that he's a thief, well, we don't have a special program for thieves. Maybe someday we will. But right now, if an addict and a thief are busted for petty theft, the thief's going back to prison. The addict will be transferred to a special program and continued on parole. He gets a second chance that he wouldn't have had before we started the special program.

And so most POs acknowledge the practical differences between placing clients in special programs and returning clients to prison:

> Well, it's just easier. It's easier to get it okayed by your supervisor for one thing. Usually you can even get your client to "volunteer." I don't believe that any of these special treatments are going to work but what else can I do? I want to avoid revocations because they're

messy and time consuming. Placing your client for treatment is the easiest way to do that sometimes.

POs are also aware of the political considerations involved in getting rid of clients: "Write up a new parole plan and then get your supervisor to sign it. For some programs, you need Mr. Chaseham's signature but that's not hard to get if you know the ropes. When you get his okay, no program can turn your client down."
Social workers employed by the special treatment programs are aware of the PO's motives for sending clients to the programs. For example, a social worker associated with a narcotic offender program complained:

> A lot of POs have the idea that this is a last-chance program, and of course, it's not. They're sending us parolees who should have been returned to prison instead. There aren't many treatable addicts here now, just screw-ups. The addicts who could benefit from our program can't get in because there's not enough room and because their POs don't want to send them here until there's no other choice. I do my best to stop these abuses but it's nearly impossible. A PO who knows how to write a persuasive case and who perhaps has some clout with the politicians can get a parolee past me very easily. I turn down a lot of applicants and then get overruled by the people upstairs. Of course, anyone recommended by Chaseham gets in. He doesn't understand the problems we have here.

The DC administration seems to be aware of the ways POs use the special treatment programs. An administrator connected with the narcotic offender program backed up this social worker's complaint: "POs think of our program as a dumping ground. They send us only the cases that are untreatable. It's a convenient way for them to get rid of the cases that cause them trouble." And referring to another treatment program, a DC official said:

> This program appeals to everyone. We were dangerously understaffed and it gave us a chance to hire more POs. It gives our research

people something to evaluate. It gives our young turks work that they see as meaningful. And last but not least, it gives all the POs a chance to get rid of their troublemakers. I'd anticipated a morale problem because the POs assigned to this program are set up as an elite unit. But the other POs don't seem to mind too much. The program gives them a chance to weed their caseloads.

Special treatment programs are ordinarily implemented as "pilot projects" and are then institutionalized if it appears that the program fills a need. This will depend upon the number of parolees serviced by the program, of course, and no special treatment program has ever been phased out for lack of business.

Finally, when threats fail, and when there are no available treatment programs, the PO may reluctantly decide to return a parolee to prison. The dilemma here is obvious. Returning the parolee to prison entails the known risk of seeking a revocation warrant and defending it in hearing. Not returning the parolee to prison entails a potentially greater risk. The PO can resolve this dilemma by "building a case" against the parolee. This process consists of creating a dossier that incorporates only incidents that are compatible with the qualities of "dangerous," revocable "criminality." When the PO builds a strong case, he minimizes his chances of "losing" the revocation hearing to the dangerous man.

There is a unity here which summarizes the "uses" of records discussed up to this point. POs will not report the incidents they observe in their caseloads because of the costs in time, effort, jeopardy, and freedom. However, the DC expects its POs to control their clients, and when a parolee cannot be controlled, the PO must "use" his records to reassert himself. The PO will first initiate records meant to threaten the parolee. Second, when threats fail, the PO will initiate records that suggest a treatable pathology. The PO can usually "use" these records to get rid of the troublesome parolee through a special treatment program. Finally, when threats have failed, and when no special treatment program is available, the PO will initiate records so as to "build a case" against the parolee. In all of these processes, the PO's motive is the control of his clients.

Using Records as Protection

So far, only the PO-parolee interaction has been considered. An equally important facet of the PO's work environment is the system of informal demands made upon him by the bureaucracy. To satisfy these demands, the PO will often "use" his records to protect himself, his supervisor, and higher DC officials.

Protection is best illustrated by an example. In early 1975, reporters for two local newspapers began an investigation of alleged mismanagement in the DC. A few disgruntled POs served as press informants and thus learned of the planned series of articles. Distorted rumors caused a near panic in more than one branch office as POs scurried about, cleaning up their files. The series turned out to be more limited and less sensational than expected, however, and within a few weeks, the only residual effect was an epidemic of writer's cramp in the branch offices. One PO described the episode this way:

> That's the only time I ever saw all nine POs in the office at the same time. We wrote a lot of paper that week. When the story hit, we were all protected. The funny thing is that the story didn't say anything bad about anyone in our office. It was a false alarm, I guess. A week later, everything was back to normal.

This incident typifies protection. Under most circumstances, POs report little or no information to the DC. But from time to time, a PO will suddenly "go by the book," reporting every incident he observes regardless of the cost. What the PO is doing is protecting himself and his superiors from some potential threat such as, in this illustration, adverse publicity.

Other researchers (e.g., Takagi, 1967; Irwin, 1970) have defined protection as the writing of records so as to demonstrate *absolute* compliance with *minimal* rules in *every* case. If the PO has a model checklist, for example, he will develop a report format which includes every item on the checklist but nothing else. When trouble arises, this format protects the PO by demonstrating his *literal* compliance with rules and regulations. The theory of protection to be presented here, however, defines this "use" of records as something that happens only in *special* cases. I will develop this theory in a roundabout way, working from the circumstances and conditions that lead to the *need* for protection. First, the data suggest that in every case, protection can be defined strictly in terms of certain *types* of parolees. For example: "The rule of thumb in my caseload is that any man can miss one report period *gratis*. I'll take that back. I've got one or two men I'd report AWOL if they were five minutes late for an appointment. They're basically dangerous men."

POs often speak of "dangerous men," but meaning generally "troublesome" parolees, as described in the last chapter. In this respect, a supervisor's comment is more revealing:

> Sometimes a violation is important because of who the parolee is. If you take your average parolee, he can get arrested on a drunk charge and that won't be too important. But suppose the parolee's a convicted cop killer. Well, for him, that's going to be an important violation. If nothing else, it's going to get in the newspapers because of who he is. Any violation that makes the papers is important. We did have a cop killer on parole out of this office once and that man couldn't sneeze without two reporters showing up here.

A PO might ignore certain violations, then, but in a few special cases where the violating parolee is a special type, might report the violation.[4]

A second situation where the *need* for protection arises is where a PO is fired or resigns. The PO who takes over the caseload has no idea where protection is needed, so he takes no chances:

> When I took this caseload over, the records were in pretty bad shape. I couldn't decipher them. The first thing I did was report eight clients AWOL. The second thing I did was to complete a dozen visitations that looked fishy to me. I wrote up two warnings out of

the twelve. The records are in good shape now, so I can take it easy. That may sound like overreaction to you but it's not. The same thing would happen if somebody took this caseload over from me tomorrow. You've got to protect yourself. You never know what kind of work the PO who had the district before you did. You don't want to get blamed for his mistakes. Also, you don't know why the last PO left. He may have been fired. If that's the case, the people downtown are going to be expecting you to come up with a lot of unreported violations. If you don't find that stuff, they're going to think that you're just as sloppy as the PO they fired.

There is a fairly consistent turnover rate among newly hired POs which generate bursts of incident reports. The important point here, however, is that the *need* for protection arises because someone *expects* the PO to discover incidents in his caseload.

Examples of the conjunction of these two factors, that is, the occurrence of special parolee types and the expectations of others, are found by examining the peculiar relationship of the DC to the parole board. As the parole board in this state is filled by executive appointment, board members often have religious, academic, labor or political backgrounds and usually have no particular allegiance to the bureaucracy. Nevertheless, the DC is subordinated to the parole board in many respects. This relationship results in a muted board-bureaucracy antagonism that can be sensed in the branch offices. A supervisor told me, for example:

The parole board could release [a murderer] and if he killed [again], we'd be the scapegoats. They cover their mistakes with *special board orders*. If they let [a murderer] go, they'd write a special order that said, "Hey, watch this guy. He's dangerous." Then afterwards they'd say, "Why didn't you watch this guy like we told you to?" They don't get blamed for releasing dangerous men. We get blamed for not following their special board orders. They use special orders to cover themselves.

This supervisor has exaggerated the problem somewhat. A *special board order* is simply a codicil to the standard parole contract which places special restrictions on the parolee. For example, an inmate might be paroled on the condition that he live in a halfway house for narcotic offenders or that he submit to psychiatric outpatient care. Nevertheless, POs, supervisors, and higher DC officials view the special order as a "red flag," warning not so much about the special problems of the parolee as about the post hoc attention likely to be paid the parolee. In other words, the parole board expects something to happen with this parolee and this expectation presents the PO with a dilemma:

> Some of these special board orders are just for the record. An order will say that a client has to report twice weekly, say, but being realistic, they can't expect me *or* the client to follow that order. What happens is that I follow the order for the first month and then I slack off. Maybe after six months I can write a request to lift the order. They'll usually grant my request but there's a catch. If I lift the order and the client screws up, my neck is on the chopping block. The thing you have to learn is which special orders are for the record and which ones are for real.

This statement of the dilemma is typical but most POs solve it by taking no chances whatsoever:

> I had a "sexually dangerous" client once. After maybe a month, I called his home at curfew and there was no answer. I reported it. Maybe that's not fair to the client but at least I'm protected. Once I report it, it's out of my hands. They can do whatever they want to but they can't come back to me six months later and ask why I wasn't doing my job. All I have to do is bring out my report and ask them why they didn't revoke the client six months earlier. Those cases are like ping-pong matches. They set me up by issuing the special order and I set them up by following it to the letter. It goes back and forth like that until they get tired. Then they'll change the order or transfer the client to a special caseload or something like that.

The practical cost of reporting such incidents is the loss of freedom. This may be a desired end in some cases, however. The loss of freedom will also limit the PO's personal liability for a "bad" decision.

The relationship between the DC and the parole board, and the subsequent *need* for protection, is actually a special case of a general phenomenon. Whenever the DC deals regularly with other bureaucracies, the interaction generates a number of demands and expectations.[5] The effects of the interaction at the lower levels of the DC are predictable. Regarding the prosecutor's office, for example, a supervisor complained: "Auslander phones my POs all the time and I don't like that. He's supposed to go through me when he has a complaint. It's not a good idea to let a PO know that the prosecutor doesn't like a parolee. Some POs are intimidated and they start harrassing the parolee." And also with regards to the prosecutor's office, a PO commented:

> You get pressure from all the agencies. Auslander's the worst because he's sneaky. If he asks about a client, you know he's checking up on you. It's like they're using that one case to judge your overall performance. What you do, of course, is interpret the rules strictly on that case. Then you're just doing your job and nobody can complain.

POs have made similar statements with regards to the courts: "Judge Kraft is hard on POs. He'll take you in his chambers and tell you how he wants you to handle the parolee. If that's not bad enough, he checks up on you later. I advise my clients to file for a change of judges when they go in front of Kraft."

Now, in general, the need for protection arises whenever POs have to deal with other bureaucracies. This includes the press, the parole board, the prosecutor, and the courts. The bureaucrats in these agencies have rigid, formal notions of how POs should handle their jobs. POs cannot routinely live up to these standards, of course. But from time to time, a PO will become aware that he is handling a special case, that is, a case that is of interest to some other agency. What this means to the PO is, first, that the outside agency will scrutinize his handling of the special case, and second, that the agency will form an opinion of his general ability solely on the basis of his performance in the special case. So to protect himself, the PO "goes by the book."

It follows from this theory that the DC will demand protection from its POs. The DC comes into contact with (and perhaps, is accountable to) outside agencies only in special cases, so the political image of the DC rests on the behavior of its POs in these cases only. Protection then is the normal "use" of records. POs who do not protect themselves risk being labeled incompetent or unrealistic with consequences implied by those labels.

Conclusion

The phenomena described here have two implications. First, parole records do not accurately reflect the behavior of parolees. This is not a novel finding, however. Bittner and Garfinkel (1967) have shown that even where record-keeping is strictly regulated, the practical costs charged to the record writer amount to "good reasons for bad records." Zimmerman's (1969; 1970) studies of public aid intake offices also point out how the practicalities of bureaucratic work shape the records produced by the office. In the area of parole itself, Prus and Stratton (1976) have specified a number of mundane considerations which enter the PO's case decisions.[6]

A second, more important implication concerns the role of the bureaucracy in these various "uses." Career contingencies in the DC are such that POs are rewarded for producing "bad" records and punished for producing "good" records. The DC realizes some political benefit from the dynamic operation of these contingencies but it does so at the price of a straightforward loss of data. That the DC can classify and process men released from prison even in a total information vacuum suggests that the DC per se makes no decisions of any consequence. Classification decisions are instead left up to the street-level bureaucrat, that is, to the PO, and to other criminal justice agencies.

The organizational outcomes or labels that emerge from this process appear to have little bearing on the statutory goals of the DC. The first outcome, "success," can be described as a nearly stochastic process. If a parolee can survive for two years without coming into contact with other criminal justice agencies, he is discharged as a "success." POs may discover behavior that is inconsistent with this outcome but career contingencies encourage the POs to suppress such data. The second outcome, "failure," is defined as the complement of the first and is likewise nearly stochastic. If a parolee cannot survive for two years without coming into contact with other criminal justice agencies, he is returned to prison as a "failure."

The two deterministic exceptions to this process are "treatable" cases and special cases. "Treatable" cases can be viewed as incipient "failures" because the PO is likely to discover a pathology only after the parolee has had an initial contact with a criminal justice agency. If it appears that further contacts will occur, the PO is encouraged to "use" his records to get rid of the parolee. Finally, in special cases, the PO must report whatever behavior he observes; or in the extreme, is expected to observe. In special cases, the PO is acting as an agent of some other bureaucracy, and as such, he is collecting information that is useful not to the DC, but to the outside agency. In special cases then, classification and processing is left up to the outside agency. By abrogating authority in these cases, interagency squabbles are avoided, and in that sense at least, the PO has protected himself and his DC superiors.

NOTES

1. Substantial portions of this chapter appeared as "How parole officers use records," *Social Problems*, 1977, *24*(5). They are reprinted here by permission of *Social Problems* and the Society for the Study of Social Problems.

2. Weber's Fifth Characteristic of a bureaucracy provides a counterpoint here. According to Gerth and Mills (1958: 198), "When the office is fully developed, official activity demands the full working capacity of the official. . . . Formerly, in all

cases, the normal state of affairs was reversed: official business was discharged as a secondary activity." A majority of the POs, in contrast, see official duties as a sideline. Over 30 percent of the POs are full time students, for example; one PO actually completed a Ph.D. while a full time employee of the DC. The DC is aware of this situation unofficially. One high DC official estimated that POs spend no more than fifteen hours per week attending to official business. Toleration here is viewed as a fringe benefit by both sides. This raises the paradox of the bureaucrat who chooses a career largely because it is *not* a career. However, if this aspect of the career is seen as a demand made upon the bureaucrat, it turns out that other demands have been substituted. The DC then defines loyalty as something other than "the full working capacity of the official." So long as the PO satisfied these other demands, his "free" time is his own to spend in any way he likes.

3. There is so little variance in this statistic that it could not be used to evaluate performance. The POs who were "promoted" during the course of this study had neither high nor low return-to-prison rates. POs nevertheless emphasize this statistic. Many POs can recite their return-to-prison rates to the third digit, and when POs have exaggerated their statistics to me, the exaggeration has always turned out to be an underestimation.

4. There seems to be a general principle here. See Emerson (1969) for a discussion of how assessments of moral character affect juvenile court decisions. Schur (1971) discusses this aspect of decision-making from a broad theoretical foundation.

5. There is a distinction here between agencies that deal routinely with the DC, the police, for example, and agencies that do not. Expectations and demands arise only in the former case. See Sudnow (1965) for a discussion of how routine dealings between a public defender and prosecutor result in normal crimes. Normal crimes emerge precisely because these two offices interact routinely and frequently.

6. These concerns are most critical in the area of program evaluation. McDowall (1976) has reviewed a number of bureaucratic case studies, concluding that program evaluation is not impossible even with "bad" records. The evaluator must be aware of the record-keeping contingencies, however. Most evaluators ignore the intervening variables, treating records as if they were a direct function of the program goals. In this sense, an evaluation is not "only as good as the records" upon which it is based, but rather, will be optimally valid when based on site-specific knowledge. This knowledge can come from a participant observer working on the evaluation team.

Chapter 6

A SOCIOLOGY OF PAROLE

In Chapter 2, I described the relationship of the branch offices (and the people who work in them: supervisors and POs) to the central authority (DC officials). Each branch office runs itself and this arrangement serves the interests of both the branch offices and the central authority. The rationale for bureaucratic federalism is that autonomous branches can respond to the immediate needs of local constituencies while still performing a greater, nonlocal function. Interagency squabbles and political feuds are avoided, so branch office autonomy serves the best interests of DC officials. To the POs and supervisors, branch office autonomy is its own reward. Each worker is free to structure his work environment to suit personal tastes, so autonomy is seen as a fringe benefit.

In Chapter 3, I listed the prices supervisors and POs pay to maintain branch office autonomy. Each PO is a potentially powerful actor at the level of the case decision. Individual exercises of power bring outsiders into the branch offices, however, and this threatens autonomy. To minimize outside scrutiny, POs behave by a set of understandings that amount to structural constraints on discretionary power. The POs enforce these unwritten rules themselves. The crux of this argument is that the *dynamic of the parole bureaucracy* runs on an autonomy incentive. So long as the branch offices run autonomously, though within a set of structural constraints, the POs benefit. When a peer tries to upset the *dynamic,* that is, when he violates an unwritten rule, he is denounced.

In Chapter 4, I began to describe how the *dynamic* shapes parole outcomes. Specifically, certain types of parolees threaten the bureaucratic status quo by making trouble for the PO and for the DC. To the PO, trouble means work and work means less free time and more structure in the work environment. To the DC administrator, trouble means friction with other criminal justice agencies. But while trouble means different things to different actors, the cause of trouble is the same: certain types of paroles. By typing the parolee at the start of the parole experience, the PO neutralizes potential trouble.

In Chapter 5, I described how these same concerns shape parole records. POs *use* records to control trouble when it arises and to eliminate potential sources of trouble before they arise. One of the most important uses of records in this respect is "protection." Other criminal justice bureaucracies have unrealistic expectations of the DC. To protect himself and his superiors, the PO must live up to these unrealistic expectations, at least on paper. Consequently, there is little direct correlation between parolee behavior, PO behavior, and official records of either.

The recurrent theme of these chapters is that POs want above all to keep outsiders from examining their performance. DC officials want above all to present a good face to the public and to other criminal justice agencies and these two interests coincide in the bureaucratic dynamic. I have called this essay "a sociology of parole." Yet these themes can easily fall into other sociological modes. For example, the sociology of deviance may be invoked to explain the processes by which some parolees become "dangerous men." I have been concerned overall with providing an alternative explanation of the parole process. Whereas classical schemes see this process as a *ceteris paribus* experiment in which men released from prison succeed or fail per se, I have described this phenomenon as a deviance process. In this sense, my argument may fall into the sociology of deviance.

Similarly, the sociology of formal organizations may be invoked to explain bureaucratic dysfunction. As I noted in the first chapter, however, it is not clear that such phenomena as the "use" of records are indeed dysfunctions. The problem here is that the DC is not a wholly integrated organization, but rather, is a dynamic organization whose goals are formed by the interactions of power groups. The DC thus has few well-defined goals as most other formal organizations do, and conversely, unlike most other formal organizations, the DC has many real and well defined goals not made explicit in a policy sense. Protection is a de facto policy of the DC, for example. Yet because it is an implicit policy, its attainment as a goal cannot be analyzed.

While constructs from both of these sociological modes are powerful in limited contexts, neither mode is exclusively and solely appropriate. The sociology of parole adapts constructs from each mode. In the largest sense, the sociology of parole addresses phenomena beyond the specific process of parole and this circumstance may be used to shed more light on the parole process. The sociology of parole is concerned first with the dynamics of "social service" bureaucracies, that is, of bureaucracies where an implicit goal is to serve the poorly defined "needs" of a client population. Second, the sociology of parole is concerned with the bureaucratic application of moral criteria to clients. In this largest sense, parole is similar to many other social processes and a study of other processes increases our basic understanding of the parole process.

In this chapter, I will compare the DC (and POs) to a public aid agency (and public aid caseworkers). Public aid is similar to parole in many respects. Public aid caseworkers are charged with satisfying the needs of aid recipients while at the same

time protecting the public coffers from welfare "cheats." Overall, the public aid agency is charged with the application of
moral labels to people much in the same way as the DC is
charged with the classification of men released from prison. But
in many important respects, there are differences between these
two phenomena and it is in these differences that we learn
about the parole process.

Becoming a PO: The Caseworker Model

Bernard Beck has pointed out a similarity between public aid
and parole bureaucracies.[1] Public aid casework (and parole
work) entails routine duties performed in the field. As there is
no direct supervision in the field, caseworkers (and POs) can
steal chunks of time by cutting corners on official duties. In an
early study of caseworkers, Bogdanoff and Glass (1954) report
that caseworkers supplement their incomes by spending this
stolen time on an "outside racket." Stolen time becomes a
fringe benefit. Caseworkers who might otherwise quit the
agency become so tied to the "outside racket" that leaving the
agency becomes unthinkable. Of course, we have seen that this
is also true of POs.

Twenty years after Bogdanoff-Glass, Forbes (1973) and
Evans (1975) studied caseworkers from the same agency, ar-
riving at similar conclusions. Bogdanoff-Glass, Forbes, and
Evans all attribute the "outside racket" phenomenon to a lack
of commitment to bureaucratic careers. The Weberian-ideal
bureaucracy controls rule-breaking by its workers through the
career.[2] The first component of a career is a course of training
which commits the future workers to the *values* of the bureaucracy. For example, a degree of social work might commit a
future worker to the values of a public aid agency. The second
component of a career is a system of graded promotions which
commits the worker to the *policies,* or realized values of the
bureaucracy. The career might be regarded simply as a socialization process whereby the bureaucracy turns out loyal, imper-

sonal bureaucrats. As caseworkers are not committed to bureaucratic careers, however, another socialization process, controlled
by a clique of rule-breakers, takes over.

The problem with caseworkers, according to Bogdanoff-
Glass, Forbes, and Evans, is that caseworkers are not committed
to bureaucratic careers either by past training or future expectations. Novice caseworkers are typically recruited from a chroni-
cally underemployed pool of liberal arts graduates. Novices take
jobs with the agency because there is nothing better available.
The job is temporary employment, a job that will be discarded
when something better comes along.

Unlike the caseworker, the novice PO enters the DC fully
committed to a bureaucratic career. Novice POs ordinarily have
some prior experience with parole work. Many worked part-
time for a parole agency before graduation. Some served as
student interns with a parole agency. All have undergraduate
degrees in social work or in a service oriented, applied social
science and a sizeable minority have degrees in "correctional
sciences."

While caseworkers and POs are similar in terms of what they
become, it appears that they started from different positions.
This does not rule out the caseworker model, however. Novice
POs are indeed committed to careers but not to the careers
offered by the DC.

The novice PO's first contact with the DC is through a civil
service job announcement. According to this announcement, a
PO "counsels and advises . . . parolees on personal, social, financial family, employment, and psychological problems. . . . Parti-
cipates in . . . programs so as to develop greater skills and
knowledge of counseling."[3]

These are the *values* the novice PO has acquired by education. The job description is a close match to his ideal career
expectations. Furthermore, the DC calls the people who hold
these jobs "parole counselors," and if the novice could *name* his
ideal career, it would not be much different than this. The
novice will soon learn, however, that there is a considerable
discrepancy between these values and DC policy. If policy is

supposed to be a set of realized values, then the DC has lied to him.

Novices are hired as probationary employees. At the end of six months, the DC will either grant him civil service tenure or fire him. The actual decision is made by a branch office supervisor and his POs, that is, by a branch office team. The branch office team has an interest in maintaining the bureaucratic dynamic, so to become a PO, the novice must become a team player.

The novice spends his first week of employment in a classroom training session. By the end of the week, he has memorized most of the important operational rules and regulations of the DC. He knows right from wrong. In the next few weeks, he works out of a branch office under the guidance of a trainer. The trainer and the novice spend a great deal of time in the field together. Trainers are ordinarily highly regarded, competent POs, so the novice will come away from this experience with a great respect for his trainer.

At the start of the second month, the novice is given a caseload of his own. He is told to work this caseload but to seek advice from his trainer whenever problems arise. The novice expects to encounter no problems but he soon learns that parole work is not as easy as it seems.

According to DC rules, a PO spends two days in the office and three days in the field every week. The novice initially wants to meet each of his parolees face-to-face. If he has one hundred clients, given twelve field days per month, he must average eight or nine contacts per day. This does not seem unreasonable. At the end of the first week, however, the novice will be lucky if he has met eight or nine of his clients. The reasons for this failure will be explained shortly.

As an aside, note that the novice's motives relate to his values. He wants to counsel his clients. A first step in this direction is a face-to-face meeting with each client where rapport is established.

Unlike the rest of the POs in his office, the novice must hand in a report within a week of each contact. As the novice has contacted eight or nine clients by the end of the first week, he must hand in eight or nine reports. He is conscious of his role as a parole counselor, so his first reports give vivid descriptions of the "personal, social, financial, family, employment, and psychological problems" of the clients he has contacted. He is quite proud of these reports, so he is shocked when his supervisor hands them back to him. All are rejected. All require "further investigation" or "more work."

The problem here, as far as the novice can see, is that his supervisor suffers from a bookkeeper mentality. If the novice makes a simple statement about a client's financial situation, the supervisor wants the statement backed up. To do this, the novice must contact the client's employer, friends, family, and landlord to corroborate the statement. Each sentence of a three page report will require ten pages of corroboration. The novice is already behind schedule with his contacts. He sees himself spending two weeks to write up a single report and this frightens him.

When he seeks his trainer's help with the reports, he is advised to keep his reports brief. Except for extraordinary situations, a report should mention only that the client was contacted. The novice knows that DC rules and regulations call for more detailed reports and he points this out to his trainer. The trainer counters this argument by pointing out the many ways in which reports can be misinterpreted by DC officials and by other criminal justice agencies. The trainer explains that a PO could do his clients a disservice by writing detailed reports. In the future, these reports could be twisted to mean something that had not been intended. To illustrate this point, the trainer may relate a story where this has happened. The trainer might also read one of the novice's verbose reports aloud, pointing out areas where the report could be misinterpreted.

His personal tastes and feelings to the contrary, the novice ends up taking his trainer's advice on this matter. It makes good sense even though it is not consistent with DC policy. The novice realizes if nothing else that his supervisor will not let him write the kinds of reports that he would like to write. And as he regards his actual counseling work as more important than paperwork, he realizes that the compromise is for the best.

As the month comes to a close, his supervisor will remind him that he is falling behind with his visitations. After discussing the matter with the novice, the supervisor calls the trainer in to help. Of course, the novice will find this humiliating but he has no choice in the matter.

The first thing the trainer will do is explain to the novice that it is impossible to make face-to-face contacts with every client every month. The novice will point out that DC regulations require this *if possible.* The trainer will counter with the argument that it is *never possible,* that no PO, not even he, could make one hundred eyeball contacts in a month. Using the phone, the novice and his trainer complete most of the remaining contacts in a single day. The relief of making the monthly deadline is some consolation to the novice but he still believes that, next month or perhaps the month after, he will be able to meet all his clients face-to-face.

Even with the help of his trainer, however, the novice may have one or two clients who have not been contacted by deadline. When he hands in the rest of his reports, his supervisor notices the missing contacts and instructs the novice to file AWOL reports for these clients. The novice explains that these clients have probably not absconded, and hence, are not AWOL. He was simply unable to contact these clients. The supervisor listens to this explanation patiently but then explains that, by law, the parolee must contact his PO, not vice versa. By law, these clients are AWOL. However, the supervisor agrees to extend the report deadline by twenty-four hours. If these clients can be contacted by then, they are not AWOL.

The novice quickly calls his trainer for help in making these contacts. The trainer suggests instead that the novice *fake* the contacts. Now the novice knows that this violates DC regulations but he is nevertheless likely to follow the advice. The moral dilemma is that if he does not break the rules, his clients will be returned to prison through no fault of their own. Despite the law, he knows that the PO ordinarily contacts the parolee, not vice versa, so it is he who has failed, not the clients. He is not morally prepared to condemn men to prison merely to cover his own failure.

Note that this is the first unambiguous violation of the rules. Prior to this time, the novice may have *felt* that he had broken a rule but each situation was ambiguous enough, and the wording of the rule ambiguous enough to permit some rationalization. In contrast, there is no ambiguity here. More importantly, the motives here were entirely altruistic. It is always easier to break a rule for a good reason than for a bad reason or for no reason at all. Later, the PO initiates fraudulent records almost as a reflex. Having once violated a rule, successive violations are easier.

The novice's first month with his own caseload is characterized by a series of traumatic shocks and disappointments. The second month will be less punishing, and in fact, may be rewarding. As the novice has already learned to write brief reports, he finds that spending two days in the office is wasteful. He could easily finish all of his reports in a single morning. On the other hand, he finds that three days in the field do not give him enough time to make all of the face-to-face contacts he would like to make. He still believes that he could make eyeball contact with his entire caseload if he were not forced to waste two days in the office.

When he mentions this to his trainer, he is advised to skip his office hours whenever possible. The novice has noticed that the other POs in the branch office do this, so he is excited. He explains (coyly) to the trainer that he would like to do this but he fears being caught and fired. The trainer explains that there is no danger of this if the novice follows simple precautions. At this point, the trainer explains the principles of the branch office team, especially the practice of *covering* which forms the social contract of the branch office. To settle the matter, the trainer agrees to speak to the supervisor on behalf of the novice.

The next day, the supervisor calls the novice in for a *tête-à-tête*. He explains that the DC rules concerning office hours are strictly advisory. For a good reason, such as emergency counseling, the novice can skip his office hours. Of course, he must check in by phone during the day in case some problem arises. And of course, there are common sense limits to this arrangement. The novice must spend enough time in the office to handle his routine duties.

This is the second unambiguous act of rule breaking. Office hours have become a dreaded chore, however, so by breaking this rule, the novice rids himself of the most boring part of his job. He may also convince himself that he is breaking the rule for a good reason. His office hours were a waste of time. In the beginning, he does not actually steal time. When he skips his office hours, he spends an equivalent amount of time in the field, trying to contact his clients.

What the reallocation of time between office and field actually does is free up his daily routine. He can take longer lunch hours if he wishes, and if some personal business comes up, say, a dental appointment, he can easily fit it into his schedule. Freedom is addictive. He begins to spend less and less time in the office, and if he feels any guilt about this, he can easily rationalize it. After all, the DC pays him to work forty hours and he does this. If he takes two hours off on Monday afternoon, he works an hour later on Tuesday and Wednesday afternoons. Or if he oversleeps one morning, he works past quitting time that afternoon.

Note that the supervisor has encouraged the novice to skip his office hours. In this respect, the PO supervisor and the caseworker supervisor differ markedly. Bogdanoff-Glass describe the casework supervisor as a Weberian-ideal bureaucrat, fully committed to the career. The casework supervisor will not tolerate rule-breaking. Forbes and Evans concur. Both suggest that the agency *selects* its supervisors on the basis of their commitments to career. We see on the other hand that the PO supervisor is an active member of the rule-breaking clique. Unlike his counterpart in the public aid agency, the PO supervisor plays a crucial role in the socialization of the novice.

There are a number of factors to explain this difference. First and most important, the DC does not appear to *select* its supervisors on the basis of commitment to career.[4] Nor is it clear that the DC sees as a "good" supervisor one who embraces the expressed values and policies of the agency. If anything, the evidence points in the other direction. A "good" supervisor, so far as the central authority is concerned, is one who runs a trouble free branch office.

Second, unlike the caseworker and his or her supervisor, the PO and his supervisor have similar interests. Overall, the strength of the dynamic is that DC officials, supervisors, and POs have a common definition of *trouble*. A "dangerous man," for example, causes trouble for all parties even though the form of the trouble may differ. In terms of socialization then, the supervisor's idea of a "good" PO is one who fits into the team. Although different words are used, DC officials see the same qualities.[5]

Third, the DC branch offices provide an optimal environment for the POs to socialize their supervisor. The point here is that the public aid agency studied by Bogdanoff-Glass, Forbes, and Evans did not have actual branch offices. Rather, a number of autonomous working units were housed under the same roof. Caseworkers accountable to different supervisors were often seated at adjacent desks whereas two caseworkers accountable to the same supervisor might have been separated by many desks, walls, and doors. For the caseworker, "branch office" is an abstract symbol on an organizational chart. For POs, "branch office" has meaning in both the organizational and physical senses. The geographic separation of the branch offices is of such magnitude that it would be nearly impossible to visit each office in a single day.

In this factor, we see an interaction between the social and physical environments. Geographic separation facilitates the development of actual teams, each with a distinctive character. A PO cannot depend on another PO in some other part of the city for advice or help, but rather, must depend on his office mates. Likewise, a supervisor cannot depend on another supervisor for advice or help, but rather, must depend on his own POs.

The difference among public aid supervisors noted by Evans can be explained partially by differential socialization or co-optation. A "bad" supervisor is one who has resisted the attempts of his workers to socialize him. Of course, the geographic separation of the DC branch offices presents an optimal environment for POs to socialize their supervisor. If the supervisor wants to leave the office early in the afternoon, he has to depend on his POs to cover him. Once he does this, his relationship to his POs changes. The geographic separation of the DC branch offices is undoubtedly the most important variable of the bureaucratic dynamic.

Another major difference between novice POs and novice caseworkers is the role of the *client* in the socialization process. Midway through his period of probationary employment, the novice PO is still trying to counsel all of his clients. He suspects that his problems in this area will shrink as he settles into his district. He has been unable to make significant face-to-face contact with the majority of his clients but he believes that this is due to his inexperience. In fact, with the exception of no more than a dozen clients who encourage his overtures, clients avoid him. The truth of the matter is that most parolees try to minimize their contact with the PO.

We may contrast this with the public aid caseworker. If an aid recipient sees his or her caseworker walking down the street, the recipient changes course and speed so as to intercept the caseworker. Aid recipients maximize their interaction with caseworkers because caseworkers control the source of wealth. The recipient increases his or her material position in the world only through interaction with the caseworker. The caseworker is ipso facto a significant other in the recipient's social world, and through maximal interaction, the recipient becomes a significant other in the social world of the caseworker. But if a parolee sees his PO walking down the street, the parolee changes course and speed so as to evade the PO. The PO is indeed a significant other in the parolee's social world, but the parolee *minimizes* his interaction with the PO, and hence, never becomes a significant other to the PO.

Both Forbes and Evans report that caseworkers break agency rules to the benefit of their clients. Eisenstadt (1959; Eisenstadt and Katz, 1960) states as a general principle that, whenever the client becomes a significant other to the bureaucrat, a process of debureaucratization ensues. The bureaucrat can no longer execute agency policy with an impersonal manner. Forbes and Evans both relate anecdotes to illustrate this phenomenon. Put simply, we may say that the aid recipients try to socialize their caseworkers in much the same way that the caseworkers try to socialize their supervisors.

Of course, the novice PO *must* maintain a businesslike, impersonal attitude towards his parolees. Should he begin to break rules in favor of his clients, the novice will not survive his period of probationary employment.[6] Fortunately, the novice has little opportunity to break rules for his clients. There are two reasons for this. First, his parolees have not become significant others to him. While he may have contacted every one of his clients by this time, the contacts have been limited, usually consisting of a brief phone conversation. The exception to this rule are the few *sincere* clients who have encouraged the novice's overtures, and thus, have become significant others to the novice.

Second, the novice will ordinarily have had a few negative experiences with clients by this time. For example, in his attempts to have face-to-face contact with every client, the novice may have provoked a client. Parolees frequently make formal "harrassment" charges against POs, and while these charges seldom lead to a disciplinary procedure, they can prove embarrassing to the PO. Or a client may have misled the novice, causing him to take some action that later proved unwarranted. Novices are always disappointed and disillusioned when they discover that a parolee has lied to them.

Another source of disappointment for the novice is his dealings with other criminal justice agencies. During the first few months of his probationary period, the novice has not had to deal routinely with the police and prosecutor. His supervisor and trainer have handled that end of the job. At some point, however, the novice feels that he can handle these duties.

With formal credentials in social work, the novice considers himself to be an expert in some areas. He expects other criminal justice bureaucrats to recognize his expertise and to give his opinions the respect they deserve. Instead he discovers that these other criminal justice bureaucrats have a low opinion of his competence. They ask him to do things that are unethical or at least inconsistent with sound rehabilitation principles. When he objects, explaining the sociological and psychological theories underlying sound rehabilitation principles, they listen politely and then repeat their requests. If he refuses to do what they ask, they go over his head. They always get what they want.

When these crises arise, the supervisor and trainer advise the novice to go along with the police and prosecutor. If the novice takes this advice he does so only to avoid extra work and to avoid making trouble for his supervisor. The trainer, who is always more cynical about these things, will explain to the novice that these other agencies can make trouble for the supervisor. But even if the novice decides to be more co-operative with the police and prosecutor, he will be humiliated by this experience.

Up to this point, my description of the socialization process has centered on the roles of trainer and supervisor. Of course, the other POs in the branch office play complementary roles. They treat the novice as an equal for the most part. They do favors for him and he does favors for them. Novices in fact are flattered when other POs ask for favors. With regard to the covering of court days,[7] for example, the other POs in the branch office may ask the novice to cover them. He does this gladly because it makes him feel a part of the branch office team, and sometimes, because he believes that winning friends in the branch office will pay off when his probationary period comes to an end. Covering court days should not trouble the novice unduly. In principle, it is the same as skipping office hours. When POs ask him to cover their court days, they explain that they have other more important duties to attend to on that day.

In addition to office mates, the "professionals" play a crucial role in the socialization process. As POs are remarkably homogeneous in terms of age, education, and attitude, it is not surprising to discover that parole work has a social dimension. There are three meeting places in the city where POs gather daily to socialize. The POs seen at these meetings are the "professionals."[8]

A clique member ordinarily attends these gatherings irregularly, usually not more than once per week or less than once per month. Typically, a member shows up when he has spent the afternoon working in the office or in the field. Novice POs attend more frequently. A novice is introduced to the "professionals" by his trainer. Thereafter, the clique encourages the novice to attend the gatherings on his own. As the members attending the gatherings change from day to day, the novice has an opportunity to meet many new POs and to learn about parole work.

The "professionals" are important to the socialization process. They may actually teach the novice certain technical aspects of rule breaking, although this is uncommon. The novice ordinarily learns these things from his trainer and supervisor. More often, the "professionals" tell myths that help explain to the novice the meanings of parole work. When a novice attends a meeting, the "professionals" will solicit his experiences and opinions. The novice relates an experience, something about parole work he does not understand. The "professionals" listen sympathetically, nod knowingly to each other, and then tell myths.

One of the most common myths is the "bag." Its telling usually follows the novice's complaints about the quality of his interactions with clients. According to the "bag" myth, certain parolees try to engineer situations where it appears that the PO is behaving dishonestly or unethically. Once the PO has been "bagged" in this way, the parolee has a weapon. He can blackmail the PO. In the future, the PO cannot make trouble for the parolee without also making trouble for himself.

There are dozens of variations to the myth of the "bag" but all have the moral: The PO must remain aloof from his caseload. Above all, the PO must never break rules to benefit the client. The client may in fact *beg* his PO to break a rule, but when the foolish PO does, he is "bagged." Underlying this moral is the norm of the sincere client. Of course, not all clients are "bag artists." The key to parole work is developing diagnostic skills that can be used to recognize the half-dozen sincere clients in a caseload. Sincere clients need help, and as they are also trustworthy, the PO can break rules to benefit his sincere clients. But be careful. There are never more than a half-dozen sincere clients in any caseload.

Another common myth concerns the "perfect case." According to this myth, Auslander, the prosecutor, tries to railroad innocent clients. Auslander does this because he is a "congenital asshole" and a would-be politician who dreams of a high elected office. Some say Governor, others say Senator. Auslander can get away with railroading innocent clients because the craven administrators who run the DC fear him and always give him what he wants. However, there is one way to stop Auslander and that is to develop a "perfect case." The "perfect case" has a ring of truth to it. Auslander knows that if he tries to run roughshod over a "perfect case," he will be made to look like a fool in federal court, and worse, in the newspapers.

The telling of this myth usually follows the novice's complaint about a humiliating experience with the prosecutor or police. Again, the "professionals" listen sympathetically, nod knowingly to each other, and then tell the myth. Every PO has a number of versions of the "perfect case" which can be told in first person singular. However, the moral varies little from version to version: Give Auslander what he wants unless you have a "perfect case."

The myth of the "perfect case" reinforces several branch office norms, all concerned with the bureaucratic dynamic. Related to these norms is a functionally similar myth, the "rep."[9] According to this myth, a PO with a strong rep for competence can deal with Auslander from a position of rough equality. Each "professional" has his own version of this myth but each has the same plot and moral: If a PO builds a strong rep in the DC and with other criminal justice agencies, he acquires power. The myth of "rep" gives the novice hope that his position, vis-à-vis the other criminal justice agencies, will improve as time passes.

In addition to myth telling, the "professionals" introduce the novice to the notion of "free" time and outside interests. A common topic of conversation at clique gatherings is a discussion of the progress various members have made in their outside interests. As most of these outside interests are related to parole work, but at a higher, more "professional" level, the novice finds them intriguing.

The modal outside interest is *education*. Many POs are working for advanced degrees in social work or a social science. These POs are constantly in the process of "writing a thesis" of some scientific import. For example, POs are doing "original research" in the areas of psychosexual criminality, personality measurement, theories of differential identification, various psychotherapies applied to criminals, and systems concepts of rehabilitation. The common theme underlying education is *specialization*. These POs want to become specialists, that is, they want to deal with only certain *types* of parolees and usually in the context of counseling or therapy.

Another common outside interest is *consulting*. A number of POs who have already earned graduate degrees work part-time for private or specialized public social service agencies. This work is usually poor paying if it pays at all, but the PO realizes substantial prestige from the work. A number of POs in this category have acquired all the trappings of the consultant, including resumes, business cards, and private offices. These POs are accorded the highest status.

As an aside, note that two POs in this category teach classes in parole related subjects at local junior colleges. This is the ultimate status goal of the consultant. Nearly every PO interviewed during the course of this study has indicated he would like eventually to teach. As the path to this goal is graduate education, the importance of this outside interest is at least partially explained. While few POs enter graduate school with the explicit intent of teaching, most want to keep this option open.

Finally, many POs do *counseling* in their "free" time. In some cases, this is synonymous with consulting. It is done through private or specialized public social service agencies and for little or no pay. Two POs have actually started informal group counseling services through the branch offices. POs refer clients to these services. A number of POs take turns leading the therapy groups and novices are invariably invited to observe the sessions.

This is undoubtedly the most important aspect of the socialization process. Novices are impressed with the high level of "professionalism" mirrored in these outside interests. Many novices intend to go on to graduate school to begin with and took jobs with the DC to earn money for this. But the "professionals" show the novice that he can attain these goals without resigning from the DC. Moreover, should the novice have any doubts about the value of graduate education, these are destroyed by the success stories told by the "professionals." Clique members serve as models in this sense, leading the novice into an outside interest. If the novice has taken preliminary steps in the direction of an outside interest during his six-month probationary period, his chances of earning civil service tenure increase. This is so because, when the novice embraces an outside interest, he must also embrace the interests of the branch office team.

Finally, we see that the socialization process for POs is more crucial to the end product than the analogous process for caseworkers. Bogdanoff-Glass, Forbes, and Evans all describe a considerable amount of variance among caseworkers. The socialization process has differential effects, creating both "good" and "bad" caseworkers as the rule breaking cliques define those terms. This difference can be attributed to a single factor. For the caseworker, socialization is accomplished by the rule breaking clique; but the decision to grant the probationary caseworker civil service tenure is made by the agency. *For the PO, both socialization and the decision to grant civil service tenure are controlled by the same party: The branch office team.* To maintain the status quo, the branch office team will not grant civil service tenure to any novice who has not been fully socialized.

Conclusion: A Sociology of Parole

POs are not caseworkers and parolees are not aid recipients but there are enough similarities to encourage generalization. Rule-breaking characterizes the official behavior of the social service bureaucrat. And while there is considerable variation, it appears that this can be explained by interactions with superiors and interactions with clients.

Bogdanoff-Glass, Forbes, and Evans all report that, from the caseworker's perspective, supervisors range from "bad" to "good." A "good" supervisor is one who tolerates rule-breaking. On the other hand, there appears to be no variance among PO supervisors. All are "good." The PO supervisors presumably varied in terms of personality at some point in their lives but the socialization process in the branch offices has had a strong homogenizing effect. Note that the physically distinct branch offices of the DC give POs an optimal situation for co-opting their supervisors. Branch office supervisors are isolated from each other, so each must rely on his POs. When they cover for him, he can no longer enforce DC policies impersonally. More importantly, the isolation of the branch office supervisors prevents them from developing into a distinct class. The interests of the branch office team are also the interests of the branch office supervisor.

Similarly, rule-breaking phenomena must vary as a function of the bureaucratic worker's ability to resist co-optation by his clients. Both Forbes and Evans report that caseworkers most frequently break rules to the benefits of their clients. POs on the other hand break rules to the benefit of clients only in the special cases of sincere clients. Otherwise the PO breaks rules only to further his personal interests.

These patterns of interaction seem to explain most of the variance in rule-breaking behavior between these two agencies. At other levels of analysis, the two agencies appear to suffer from the same dysfunction and for the same reason. Weber (1958: 234) notes that, "The Russian czar . . . was seldom able to accomplish permanently anything that displeased his bureaucracy and hurt the power interests of the bureaucrats." And this the root of the parole experience. While men released from prison no doubt have some control over their own destinies, parole outcomes are shaped in the main by the likes and dislikes of bureaucrats.

Earlier chapters described the processes by which bureaucrats were able to enforce their wills on the agency. As there is little comparable material in the published literature, and as many of these processes would have escaped the attention of casual observers, these earlier chapters were necessary to the sociology of parole. In this chapter, I described in very general terms how novice POs come to have likes and dislikes with respect to the outcome of paroles. After all, why should a novice PO care one way or the other about the outcome of a *ceteris paribus* experiment?

Yet it is clear from the earlier chapters that POs do have a personal stake in the outcome process and the sociology of parole must be able to explain how these interests are formed. The socialization process described in this chapter provides a minimal answer. The PO-caseworker analogy adds another dimension to the explanation. We see that the socialization process is less crucial to the bureaucratic dynamic of the DC than it is to public aid agency. Bogdanoff-Glass, Forbes, and Evans all describe a considerable amount of variance among caseworkers. Sometimes the socialization process fails and a "bad" caseworker, as defined by the rule-breaking cliques, slips through. This never happens in the DC, however, and for one reason. Caseworkers are socialized by the rule-breaking clique but the decision to grant a caseworker tenure is made by the agency. In contrast, the rule-breaking cliques in the DC control not only the socialization of novice POs, but also the tenure decision-making process. The branch office team must maintain the status quo at any cost, so it will deny tenure to any novice who has successfully resisted the socialization process.

In this respect, the branch offices are the "perfect" bureaucracies described by Gordon et al. (1974) as mysterious, self-serving "boxes." The perfect bureaucracy should be organized along four dimensions which include (1) the creation of need, (2) the management of clientele, (3) the control of information, and (4) the public perception of the agency. Of course, all four of these dimensions are found to some extent or another in the bureaucratic dynamic or status quo of the DC. With respect to (1) the creation of need, for example, we see that POs may inflate or deflate the size of their caseloads. Because the practice of "papering" caseloads is so widespread, it is nearly impossible to estimate the actual number of parolees in the city. Parolees are discharged much sooner or much later than normal so that POs can create the statistical impression of need in their caseloads. In theory, a PO could have *no* parolees in this district for as long as a year before this would become apparent to the DC.[10]

Now the long range trend in parole outcomes is in the direction of success, or at least, is not in the direction of failure. In nearly every jurisdiction, recidivism rates fall predictably from year to year. Whereas in past years the majority of all men released from prison failed on parole, the majority now succeed. There are many plausible explanations for this trend, not the least of which is the proliferation of semioutcomes. What of the parolee who is transferred from a supervision caseload to a halfway house due to alcoholism? Previously, this parolee would have been returned to prison, counted in the statistics as a failure. But now he is counted as a success at least for the duration of his stay in the halfway house.

This change in the social meaning of parole outcome is more than a simple change in bookkeeping, however. The proliferation of alternative outcomes reflects the growing complexity of parole. With a more complex role, the parole agency becomes more susceptible to the forces of status quo. The duties of the PO become so complex that the agency cannot evaluate the performance of individual POs. As the power of the branch office teams grow (inexorably), the bureaucratic dynamic evolves. DC officials are able to control the status quo only in an either/or fashion. Policy can be enforced only under the ultimate threat and few issues are important enough to warrant a confrontation.

In the long run situation, complexity overwhelms the agency. DC officials introduce complexity into the environment as a means of social control. Policy can be enforced simply by making noncompliance the more complex alternative. Complexity is defined in terms of ritual, paperwork, and formalism and POs will ordinarily choose an alternative that minimizes these factors. But complexity for its own sake or as a means of social control indicates some dysfunction in the agency. There should be more direct methods of enforcing policy.

It is also clear that the increasingly complex nature of parole is at least in part responsible for dwindling recidivism rates. It will generally be more difficult to change a parolee's status than to leave it as is, and as the parole agency becomes more formalized and bureaucratized, this factor increases. In the public aid agency, caseworkers find it easiest to keep recipients at the current level of aid. To change the level of aid, an increase or decrease, the caseworker must complete a series of investigations and written justifications. To maintain the current level of aid, in contrast, the caseworker need do nothing. During a wildcat strike at the aid agency, according to Evans, aid checks continued to be mailed out to recipients. The clerical workers who remained at their jobs during the strike simply copied old reports, changing nothing but the dates. If all aid recipients were kept at a current level of aid, then, caseworkers would have no work at all to do.[11]

If this is the trend, there is no reason to believe that it will reverse itself in the near future. Parole will become more complex and the parole agency will become more like a self-serving "black box" in order to accommodate this complexity. A direct measure of complexity can be seen in the quantity and quality of proprietary interests in each parole outcome. We have seen, for example, that other criminal justice agencies often hold proprietary interests in the outcome of certain cases. The clearest example of this might be a case involving a police informant. The police have a proprietary interest in the success of such parolees and the DC will ordinarily go along with this interest. DC officials always find it easiest to abrogate decision-making authority when other agencies express proprietary interests in a decision. DC officials per se have no personal interests or involvement in case outcomes, so there is no resentment. By abrogating authority in these cases, DC officials relieve themselves of personal culpability for "wrong" decisions. Similarly, in the public aid agency, administrators are always reluctant to modify Federal eligibility criteria even when there is some basis for a small modification or interpretation. Unlike the caseworker, administrators have no personal interest or involvement in individual case outcomes. There is nothing to be gained personally by making a decision but there is some personal risk. It is easier and safer to simply accept the Federal guidelines.

Rigidity of this type has always characterized bureaucratic behavior but it approaches dysfunction when change is the nature of the bureaucratic task. The parole agency is expected to monitor change and to affect a change in status when appropriate. Unfortunately, the agency's performance depends upon a well defined, simple role in the criminal justice system. This role becomes more complex as time passes. With respect to proprietary interests in parole outcomes, for example, it is clear that the role of the supervision agency has become overwhelmingly complex. The future of parole appears to be in the direction of greater complexity, and thus, the performance of the agencies cannot improve. Fortunately we will not have to witness this terminal dysfunction. As the role of the agency becomes more complex, the agency must become more and more self-serving, more and more like the perfect machine.

If the sociology of parole offers any recommendations, it must be to make the role of the supervision agency simpler. The agency should supervise and nothing else. The bureaucrats who perform these routine tasks should be selected for their *ability* to perform the tasks as measured in the most direct manner. Bureaucrats should not be selected on the basis of credentials or of other secondary measures of ability. Eschew professionalism and eschew complexity. Describe the role of the agency precisely and then design a bureaucracy along those functions.

NOTES

1. Personal communication, 1977.

2. I use Gerth and Mills (1958) as the source.

3. This is taken from a state civil service description of *Correctional Parole Counselor I,* dated 1971 but still in force.

4. Cf., Chapter 2, *The Supervisors;* also, Chapter 2, note 7.

5. Cf., Chapter 3. DC officials consistently speak of "good" POs as those who have good relations with other criminal justice bureaucracies.

6. Cf., Chapter 3, *The Mystique of Rep.* A PO must be *selective,* that is, he can work as an advocate for only a few clients.

7. Cf., Chapter 3, *Competence.* POs save two or three work days each month by covering each other. This practice forces POs to depend on each other, thus strengthening the sense of community. The novice typically does not care whether his favors are reciprocated because he does not yet see court days as a boring chore. However, his office mates will insist on returning the favor. When the novice skips his court days, that is, when he permits his office mates to cover for him, he begins to accept the values of the branch office team. At first, however, he permits himself to be covered only because he does not want to insult his office mates or to seem peculiar. Later, when court days lose their novelty for him, reciprocal covering takes on a more concrete aspect.

8. Cf., Chapter 2. The "professionals" are relatively powerless but they nevertheless play an important part in the (socialization) process.

9. Cf., Chapter 3.

10. Cf., Chapter 2 and note 15. Gordon et al. are speaking more to the macroconcerns. As an example of this, note that DC officials encourage POs to divert parolees to the special treatment caseloads. This inflates the importance of the program and guarantees its refunding.

11. And this is the status quo of the public aid agency. When aid recipients are kept at a constant level of aid, both the caseworkers and the agency administrators are happy. I will modify this statement shortly. However, Bogdanoff-Glass, who studied the aid agency in the 1950s, describe how caseworkers "train" their clients to accept the status quo. Once a client has been trained, the caseworker can do less work.

BIBLIOGRAPHY

BECKER, H.S. (1963) *Outsiders: Studies in the Sociology of Deviance.* Glencoe, IL: Free Press.

BITTNER, E. and H. GARFINKEL (1967) " 'Good' organizational reasons for 'bad' clinical records," in H. Garfinkel, *Studies in Ethnomethodology.* Englewood Cliffs, N.J.: Prentice-Hall.

BLAU, P. (1963) *The Dynamics of a Bureaucracy.* Chicago: University of Chicago Press.

BOGDANOFF, E. and A.J. GLASS (1954) The Sociology of the Public Case Worker in an Urban Area. M.A. Thesis, Department of Sociology, University of Chicago.

COLEMAN, J.S. (1973) *The Mathematics of Collective Behavior.* Chicago: Aldine.

COOK, T.D. and D.T. Campbell (1977) *The Design and Analysis of Quasi-Experiments in Field Settings.* Chicago: Rand-McNally.

EISENSTADT, S.N. (1959) "Bureaucracy, bureaucratization, and debureaucratization." *Administrative Science Quarterly* 4.

––– and E. KATZ (1960) "Some sociological observations on the response of Israeli organizations to new immigrants." *Administrative Science Quarterly* 5.

EISENSTEIN, J. and H. JACOB (1976) *Felony Justice.* Boston: Little, Brown.

EMERSON, R.M. (1969) *Judging Delinquents.* Chicago: Aldine.

EVANS, D. (1975) Occupational Identity and Welfare Reform: A Study of Caseworkers in the Cook County Department of Public Aid. Ph.D. Dissertation, Department of Sociology, Northwestern University.

FORBES, R.P. (1973) Socialization of the Public Caseworker: Resolution of Uncertainty. Ph.D. Dissertation, Department of Sociology, University of Chicago.

GERTH, H.H. and C.W. MILLS (1958) *From Max Weber: Essays in Sociology.* New York: Oxford University Press.

GLASER, D.T. (1964) *The Effectiveness of a Prison and a Parole System.* Indianapolis: Bobbs-Merrill.

GOLD, R. (1958) "Roles in sociological field observations." *Social Forces* 36.

GORDON, A., M. BUSH et al. (1975) "Beyond need: toward a serviced society," in *The Crime of Peace.* London: Penguin.

GOULDNER, A.W. (1954) *Patterns of Industrial Bureaucracy.* Glencoe, IL: Free Press.

IRWIN, J. (1970) *The Felon.* Englewood Cliffs, N.J.: Prentice-Hall.

179

McCLEARY, R. (1975) "How structural variables constrain the parole officer's use of discretionary power." *Social Problems* 23 (2).

––– (1977) "How parole officers use records." *Social Problems* 24 (5).

McDOWALL, D. (1977) Notes on the Use of Official Records. Mimeo, Department of Psychology, Northwestern University.

MERTON, R.K. (1949) *Social Theory and Structure.* Chicago: Modern Franklin.

––– (1940) "Bureaucratic structure and personality." *Social Forces* 35.

OLSON, M. (1965) *The Logic of Collective Action.* Cambridge, MA: Harvard University Press.

PRUS, R. and J. STRATTON (1976) "Parole revocation and decision-making: private typings and official designations." *Federal Probation* 40 (1).

QUINNEY, R. (1975) *Criminology.* Boston: Little, Brown.

SCHUR, E.M. (1971) *Labeling Deviant Behavior.* New York: Harper and Row.

SELZNICK, P. (1949) *TVA and the Grass Roots.* Berkeley: University of California Press.

SUDNOW, D. (1965) "Normal crimes: sociological features of the penal code in a public defender office." *Social Problems* 12 (2).

SUTHERLAND, E.H. and D.R. CRESSY (1970) *Criminology.* New York: J.B. Lippincott.

TAKAGI, P.T. (1967) Evaluation Systems and Deviations in a Parole Agency. Ph.D. Dissertation, Stanford University.

––– and J. ROBISON (1968) Case Decisions in a State Parole System. Sacramento: Research Division, California Department of Corrections.

ZIMMERMAN, D. (1969) "Record-keeping and the intake process in a public welfare agency," in S. Wheeler (ed.), *On Record.* New York: Russell Sage.

––– (1970) "The practicalities of rule use," in J. Douglas (ed.), *Understanding Everyday Life.* Chicago: Aldine.

ABOUT THE AUTHOR

RICHARD McCLEARY is an Assistant Professor of Criminal Justice at Arizona State University, Tempe. He received his Ph.D. in Sociology from Northwestern University in 1977. Dr. McCleary has published extensively in the areas of parole, program evaluation, and measurement. His articles have appeared in such journals as *Social Problems, Social Issues, Social Science Research,* and *Evaluation Quarterly.*